When They Invited Me to Fellowship, I Thought They Meant a Cruise

Le Blanc

When They Invited Me to Fellowship, I Thought They Meant a Cruise

by

Mark Littleton

CHRISTIAN PUBLICATIONS
CAMP HILL, PENNSYLVANIA

Christian Publications
3825 Hartzdale Drive, Camp Hill, PA 17011

The mark of 🕇 *vibrant faith*

ISBN: 0-87509-496-1
LOC Catalog Card Number: 92-81349
© 1992 by Mark Littleton
All rights reserved
Printed in the United States of America

92 93 94 95 96   5 4 3 2 1

Cover illustration
© 1992, Ron Wheeler

Scripture taken from the HOLY BIBLE: NEW
INTERNATIONAL VERSION. Copyright © 1973, 1978,
1984 by the International Bible Society. Used by permission of
Zondervan Bible Publishers.

*To
the folks I work with at MHI:
Betty, Bev, Wendy, Becky, Terri,
Alan, Dieter, Roy, Paul, Chuck, Bob, Brod,
Don, Mike, Hank, Randy,
Bill G., Bill F., Bill S., Bill W., Danny, Dave,
Nobuhara-san, Nagase-san, Sugimura-san,
Hirakawa-san,
and my dad, Richard Littleton.
You've put up with a lot
of my staring into space
and thinking about the next book.
Well, this is it.
Thanks for bearing with me.*

Contents

Introduction

How should we treat our brothers and sisters in Christ?

More importantly, how can we begin to enjoy biblical fellowship—not just donuts and coke in the church basement, or chatter at the football game, or some laughs in the bunkroom on a retreat—but fellowship, the kind that God intends us to have?

I often think about these questions when I go to church, hurry in and out of classes, pause to say hello in the hall, rush to church worship, then quickly shake the pastor's hand on the way out the door, muttering something about a helpful message this morning. Sometimes I think I had closer relationships with my poker buddies in my "B.C." days as we played five card draw, Baseball and Anaconda.

Even with my fraternity brothers in college shortly before I became a Christian I spent rousing times dicussing some of the most important issues in life—what happens when you die, whether there was a God, who Jesus Christ was, what life was all about, what kind of careers we were headed towards. Of course, we had few of the satisfying answers back then that I have now. But sometimes I long for those days when we bared our souls, deeply embroiled in a "bull session."

Even in my first years as a Christian there was intimacy and depth in my relationships.

But somehow that can all pass away. We rush through life like a train on a circular track, stopping only a few moments at each platform, then whizzing off down the rails desperate to reach the next destination.

Is this how it's supposed to be?

I think not. And that's why I've written this book, to explore what it means to develop Christian fellowship that builds relationships. In it, we'll look at 12 elements of true fellowship through studying the "one another" concepts found in Scripture.

What are the "one another" concepts?

If you read the letters of Paul, you'll find he frequently refers to things like loving one another, serving one another, encouraging one another. Paul alone uses the expression over 30 times. But you'll also find it in the writings of James, Peter and John and the words of Jesus. It's an important concept. It involves relating one to the other in ways you'll never find in the outside world.

But how are we to relate?

If you look at the typical church youth group, you'll find that much of our time together is spent listening to someone teach, sitting around in groups and sharing thoughts or chatting in the hall-ways and foyer for a moment between meetings.

Is this all our relationships are to be built on?

Scripture answers with a resounding no. God longs that we experience much deeper intimacy and love. But how? When? And where?

If you decide you want to answer those questions, read on. That's what this book is all about.

1

Getting That Good Feeling of Belonging

For just as we have many members in one body and all the members do not have the same function, so we, who are many, are one body in Christ, and individually members one of another.

Romans 12:4-5, NASB

MONDAY: Nerd country

HEART: Note found in a pew after everyone had cleared out. Two different styles of handwriting. Probably a conversation between two girls, ninth grade or so. Maybe the sermon was a little boring.

> When do you get your braces off?
>
> Soon, I hope. Why do we have to put up with this stuff?
>
> You know what they say—"You'll appreciate it when you grow up."
>
> Always "when we grow up." I'm sick of that line.
>
> So what about Eric? Are you going to dump him?
>
> Not yet. Not until Craig shows some interest.

He's after Sherry Watts.

He is not.

You think he's cuter than Eric?

Of course. Eric's . . . I don't know. I'm tired of him. He loves his computer.

I can't believe you say that. You've been going out with him for three months.

Three months too long.

Come on . . . Hey look at that Bob Nesbie in the second pew. Now there's a nerd. I can't believe the way he combs his hair.

This whole church is nerd country.

So when do you get your braces off?

Is this sermon ever going to end?

SOUL: Ever take a long look around at the people in your youth group and come to the conclusion that "this church is nerd country"?

You may be surprised to learn an important doctrine of Scripture found in Romans 12:4-5: we are "members one of another." All of us in the body of Christ are somehow—in God's eyes—joined to one another. Connected. On the same team. No—more than that. We're a single organism, parts of a body, the body of Christ.

Like the human body, the church is Christ's flesh and blood. Some of us may be arms, some legs, some eyes and ears, but we're all part of something bigger.

It's a whole new way of thinking. Many of us may regard others in the church as acquaintances, competitors, even enemies—and sometimes "nerds"—

but that's not what God intends.

MIND: Read through Romans 12:3-21 and note the number of times Paul refers to actions designed to meet the needs of others. What needs do you see listed? What ones do you recognize you have? What ones might you see another Christian as having?

MIGHT: Just as the brain commands the hand to pick up the fork and put a slice of turkey into the mouth, so all the members of the church are to function cooperatively, working towards the same ends and goals. Think of several ways you can begin to cooperate and build a sense of unity in your youth group. List two and begin doing one today.

TUESDAY: I can't do it without you.

HEART: Sylvester Stallone has immortalized two characters in the public psyche: Rocky and Rambo. Both are underdogs. Both go up against insurmountable odds. Both fight back hard. And win! They capture our hearts because they refuse to give up.

But one thing has always troubled me about both of them: they're loners. What they do they do well, but they rarely do it with anyone else. They take the shots; they also get the glory. They're the classic Lone Rangers of the 80s.

Still, there's one scene I've always loved that was featured in the second Rocky movie. Rocky's wife Adrienne refuses to agree to Rocky's fighting

Apollo Creed a second time. She believes he could lose his eyesight. They have the money. They have a home. They'll soon have a baby.

But as Adrienne argues with Rocky, Apollo Creed cranks up the campaign to get Rocky into the ring. He takes out ads in the papers that picture Rocky as the "Italian Chicken" because he won't fight. One night Rocky argues with Adrienne, "I never asked you to stop being a woman. Don't ask me to stop being a man." He flexes his muscles, stomps out of the house and tries to prepare without her support. But she's gouged out his heart. He can't do it. Not on his own, anyway.

Then Adrienne suffers an accident. She sinks into a coma. Rocky and Mick, his trainer, wait in the hospital room praying that she'll revive. In the interim Rocky decides that he won't fight. He's hurt her badly and he can't continue.

The scene unfolds and Adrienne revives after many days of tense waiting. After she does wake up, Rocky informs her he won't fight. It's then that Adrienne utters the heart-transforming line, "There's only one thing I want to you to do: Win. WIN!"

The music jolts and Rocky marches out—to win.

SOUL: Rocky couldn't do it without his wife's support.

That's an important element of what it means to be members of one another: no one can function alone; all of us need one another.

Paul brings that out in First Corinthians 12 where he discusses a problem the Corinthians were having. Some folks thought that because they had certain showy, vocal gifts they didn't need other members of the church. Paul tells them, "The eye cannot say to the hand, 'I don't need you!' and the head cannot say to the feet, 'I don't need you!' On the contrary, those parts of the body that seem to be weaker are indispensable"(1 Corinthians 12:21-22).

Like Rocky, many of us tend to think we can go it alone. We'll get that position on the yearbook. We'll win that spot on the starting lineup. But that's not the principle. We all need one another, even the ones who seem to have little or no involvement or importance.

MIND: Read First Corinthians 12:15-26, paying particular attention to Paul's emphasis on the need each member of the body has for one another.

MIGHT: You'll never "need" someone you don't know. Nor will you care much for someone whom you never talk to or listen to. What can the youth in your church do to begin talking to and listening to one another? Sit down with a friend in your group and talk about your need for one another. Tell him or her specifically what you appreciate about him or her, and what helped you in the last few weeks.

WEDNESDAY: No one more important than the other

HEART: Eight little notes. They make up a musical scale. Most music written in key uses those same eight notes in different octaves over and over.

But what if one of those notes was missing?

Imagine coming into church and the pianist sits down to play "O For a Thousand Tongues to Sing," but the A-flat is missing. He begins to play, but when you sing the first "O" it's followed by two blanks. No A-flat. "O-blank-blank-thousand tongues to-blank-my great Redeemer's praise, the glories of-blank-blank-and King, Blank-uh, tri-blank-blank His blank!"

Now wasn't that a wonderful rendering of the famous hymn?

Let's try it another way. What if the only note we could use was the A-flat? We'd sound something like this: "Blank-for a-blankety blank-blank-blank-sing, Blank-blankety-blank-blank-blank, Blank-blank-blank-blank-my God-blank-blank, Th-blank blanky-umphs-of-blank-grace!"

Wow! An enjoyable time in worship today, wasn't it?

SOUL: All that to make a point about being members of the body of Christ. And that's this: everyone's important. Paul put it this way: "If the foot should say, 'Because I am not a hand, I do not belong to the body,' it would not for that reason cease to be part of the body. And if the ear should say, 'Because I am not an eye, I do not belong to the body,' it would not for that reason cease to be part of the body"(1 Corinthians 12:15-16).

Being important in word only is one thing. But making someone feel important is quite another.

How do you "make" someone feel important, help them feel they matter in the body? One way is simply by listening to them when they talk.

There's a story about a college psychology class in which the students agreed to see if their responses to the instructor would influence his style of teaching. They decided that they'd perk up and listen whenever he stood near the wall heater and spoke in a high-pitched voice, hunched over and toying with his pipe. Whenever the prof veered away from those mannerisms, everyone looked down, acted bored, yawned and so on. But when he walked close to the heater, spoke in a high-pitched voice and so on, they jerked alert, bright and bug-eyed.

In a matter of days that class had that old prof hunched over on the heater and addressing them in a high-pitched voice, all the while fingering his pipe nervously. Remarkable!

Just the way you listen to someone packs some wallop.

MIND: How important do you feel as a member of the body of Christ? Read First Corinthians 12:14-27 again with an eye to your own place in the body. Then read Paul's comments in Second Timothy 4:9-13 for some of Paul's feelings about others in the body.

MIGHT: Feeling that you're an important member of something is critical to a strong self-image and the conviction that you're part of a team. What can you do today to make someone feel they're important to you? Offer a compliment? Write a note of thanks for a job well done? Give a small gift or card that says "I appreciate you"? Think of one person and one thing to do that will say, "You're important to me. Thanks for being part of my world."

THURSDAY: Whatever you do, don't let them unify!

HEART: Ever heard of Wormwood and Screwtape? C.S. Lewis made them famous. There's another demonic duo you might not know about: Scrubdub and Loopole. Loopole's the head of a demon team working on a local youth group. Scrubdub is his mentor, or should I say, his tor-mentor. He wrote this:

HELL-O-GRAM

Loopole:

Sounds like you've got a problem. Unity is the worst sort of situation for a tempter. Any time a group of Christians starts working together, there's bound to be rubble in the Kingdom Below. But stoke up a little jealousy, blow a bit of selfish smoke into their nostrils, and usually the problem is solved.

Your difficulty is that their youth leader's teaching them about jealousy and selfishness. And the bipeds are taking it seriously. What to do?

This Carol Briggs sounds like the wicket. A mouth for gossip, eh? That's the plot. Get her on the phone today—the minute after you get this Hell-o-gram—and have her hit up one of the young biddies for a few yards of exaggeration, a white lie or two and a full dish of the latest on "you know who." (Pick the guy and girl in the group who everyone's hoping will get together).

You know what I mean—groom her, humor, rumor, boom her.

You can do it.

Scrubdub

SOUL: Unity—one of the most difficult things to create in any church situation. Everyone has an opinion, a different slant on things, a better idea. Yet, if we're all members of the same body, we've got to get moving in the same direction. Imagine a person whose brain wants to go north while his feet scream south, and the hips yell, "Not us, we're headed east and west." That person will either blow up or crumple up in frustration.

But get everyone moving in the same direction, detonated by the same goals, and for the same Lord—and then you've got something.

That's precisely what Jesus wants of us. Listen to His words in His prayer in John 17:20-21: "My prayer is not for them alone. I pray also for those who will believe in me through their message, that all of them may be one, Father, just as you are in me and I am in you. May they also be in us so that the world may believe that you have sent me."

MIND: Look at several Scriptures on the subject of unity: First Corinthians 1:10, 12:12; Ephesians 4:3. What do these tell you about unity and what might keep you from it?

MIGHT: How can you foster unity in your church? Go back to the letter we started off today's reading with. What was it that Loopole was told to use to destroy the unity in the body? It's gossip, isn't it?

Nothing kills unity like gossip—everyone spreading rumors, digging up each other's dirt, stabbing another member in the shoulder blade. Listen to yourself and to what others say to you today. Make an effort today to say only those things that will build up the body, not tear it down.

FRIDAY: Use your gifts

HEART: It's Christmas day. You sneak downstairs just to look—an hour or two before Mom and Dad are up. You wonder what you got, if they bought you that special gift.

Finally everyone's up. It's time to sit down around the tree and open your presents. Dad goes first. He opens a huge box. No one seems to know where it came from. Inside is a huge placard that says, "The gift of administration." He holds it up for all to see. There underneath the word is an organizational chart of a family. And then suddenly it's gone—poof. Dad shakes his head and looks around. "I don't get it."

Now it's Mom's turn. She's got a big box, too. She opens it. It's another placard. This one is labeled, "Helps." It pictures a garden and a gardener. She starts to pick it up and poof! Vanished!

Everyone laughs. "Someone's playing a joke on us."

Then it's Sis's turn. She opens up her box. Her placard says "Encouragement." There's a photo-

graph of a woman sitting on a bed talking to someone. And then, zappo! It's gone, too.

Now it's your turn. You're almost afraid to open the
box up. But you do. It says "Teaching," and sure
enough there's another scene of some person at a
blackboard. But—whacko—it's gone, too.

Dad says, "I don't know what's going on here, but
let's organize the rest of the presents so we don't
lose anything."

Mom gets up and starts sorting them.

Sis sits back and laughs. "Mom, you wrapped
these gifts so nicely."

And suddenly you get it. "Hey, everyone, these are
spiritual gifts. Each one of us has been given a special gift for serving in the body. Dad's is administration—that's the ability to get things organized.
Mom's is helps—she has the special capacity for
helping others. Sis's is encouragement."

"And yours is telling us what it all means, I suppose," said Dad with a laugh.

You smile. "I guess so."

SOUL: There's been a lot written about spiritual
gifts in the body in recent years. But for most of us,
"discovering" those gifts isn't as simple as opening
a package at Christmas.

There are two important principles about spiritual
gifts in the Scriptures. One is that you have one or
several in a special combination configured by the
Spirit of God. The second is you don't have to worry
about "discovering" them. You simply get involved in
things in the church and soon you'll find out what

jobs you have a special knack for that others may not. Everyone will notice. The only way anyone can see what your gifts might be, though, is if you get out and start doing what people do. It'll be evident as you go along.

MIND: Being "members of the body" means we all have different functions, different things to do—just as ears hear and eyes see. Read the following four sections of Scripture about spiritual gifts and think through the things you may have a special capacity for. They may be your gifts. First Corinthians 12:28-30; Romans 12:6-8; Ephesians 4:11-12; First Peter 4:10-11.

MIGHT: The way to "discover" how you fit in the body of Christ and what gifts you have is not through self-analysis, or taking a spiritual test. It's through growing, maturing, and practicing the principles of Scripture. You learn to do by doing. Gradually, you'll see yourself "fitting in" in a way orchestrated by the Spirit of God. What do you like to do? Perhaps that's the very gift God's given you. Go out and use it a bit—see how you feel about it then!

SATURDAY/SUNDAY: "I have lost a brace of kinsmen!"

HEART: In the final scene of Shakespeare's famed play, *Romeo and Juliet,* all has gone wrong. Juliet lays lifeless over the body of her beloved Romeo. Both are dead. They fell in love while their families feuded and fought. They were "starcrossed" lovers, caught in a dilemma: they loved each other, but their families were mortal enemies. What could they do? Their friend the local friar cooked up a great ruse: Juliet would take a special potion and appear to die. After her burial, Romeo would return from exile just as she woke up and they would flee elsewhere, to live happily ever after.

But the plan failed. The friar didn't get word to Romeo quickly enough. He really thought Juliet was dead. When he arrived at her tomb, she appeared dead even though drugged. In despair, he drank a vial of poison. When Juliet awoke, her lover lay crumpled beside her byre. Moments later, she plunged a dagger into her heart.

When all was discovered, the friar told the story of the starcrossed lovers. But the prince summed it up with these terrible words:

> *Where be these enemies? Capulet! Montague!*
> *See what a scourge is laid upon your hate,*
> *That heaven finds means to kill your joys with*
>   *love.*
> *And I for winking at your discords too*
> *Have lost a brace of kinsmen. All are punish'd.*

SOUL: "All are punished!"

What immortal words. Two families tearing each other to pieces in the streets of their city. Two lovers, each from an enemy family, trying to find a way to seal their love without destroying their lives. Both end up dead. "All are punished."

In a way, the same thing often happens in our churches, in our youth groups. Rivalries begin. Rumors spread. Lines are drawn. A battle starts.

But aren't we members of the same body? Does it make sense for a hand to gouge a hole in a foot? Isn't it suicide for the teeth to bite a thigh?

Of course! But we don't see it that way, because we don't usually see ourselves as "members" of a body—Christ's body.

MIND: We've spent the last week looking at the fact that we're members of Christ's body. Think about it one more time. Do you see your friends and neighbors in church as part of the grand, perfect body of Christ? Or are they rivals, competitors, enemies? Read First Samuel 24:1-22 for some insight into how David looked upon a man who sought to hurt him. What advice might David offer to us in the church today who struggle against one another rather than with one another?

MIGHT: Is there someone in your youth group whom you simply do not get along with? Pray for them today. Be specific about three blessings for them that you'd want in your life. Pray about it every day for the next week. See how you feel about them after praying for them. Write down those feelings here:

_____

_____

_____

2

Mom, Why Can't They Like Me Just the Way I Am?

Accept one another, then, just as Christ accepted you, in order to bring praise to God.

Romans 15:7

MONDAY: Let him in!

HEART: When Marty walked up to the church with his two friends, Rudy and Tim, he didn't expect such a procedure. But Rudy had invited him to come. So he figured he'd at least give it a try. Then two teens stalked out at him on either side of a hulking man they addressed as "Youth Pastor."

"Checkout drill ready?" barked Youth Pastor.

"Drill ready, sir," said the two teens. They grabbed Marty at each armpit and held him. Marty didn't know whether to struggle or just be still. Both of the young men had grips like Arnold Schwartzenegger.

"Haircut!" said Youth Pastor. "Over two inches?"

One of the teens pulled out a ruler. "Under two inches, sir."

19

"Check," said the other teen.

"Ears!" seethed Youth Pastor. "Any signs of metal?"

Both teens jerked Marty by the earlobes.

"No sign, sir!"

"No sign, SIR!"

"Check!"

"Check!"

"Jacket!" boomed Youth Pastor. "Washed Denim?"

The two teens inspected the jacket under a magnifying glass.

"Washed Demin, sir. Check!" yelled both of them.

"Socks!" shouted Youth Pastor. "Color?"

The two teens jerked up Marty's pants. There was a sudden gasp. With a shudder, both teens dropped his pantlegs down over his loafers.

"SOCKS!" yelled Youth Pastor. "COLOR?"

The two teens murmured, "Black, sir."

"I can't hear you!"

"BLACK, SIR!"

Youth Pastor stared at Marty. A snarl curled onto his lips. He then glared at the two others. "You brought this thing to our youth group!" he shouted.

Rudy and Tim stared down at the sidewalk in anguish.

Youth Pastor glared at Marty. "You come here wearing black socks!" he yelled. "Away with you!" He threw his hands out in a gesturing shove.

Marty fell back and moved away from Youth Pastor. Rudy and Tim just shook their heads and shrugged, then disappeared into the halls of the church.

SOUL: "Ridiculous!" you say?

Of course.

But not something that doesn't happen on a smaller scale, in a more subtle way, in nearly every human gathering you'll find. A number of people receive acceptance or rejection on the basis of their dress, or their looks, or the way they comb their hair, or . . . you name it—there are a million variations. Every group has its own list.

Compare that attitude to one of Paul's primary commands to all of us: "Accept one another" (Romans 15:7). The word means "receive" or "take into one's home." It was used of taking food into your mouth, of receiving someone into a group and of taking along someone as a companion on a trip. In each case, it's a picture of open-armed, open-hearted love and friendship.

MIND: Get some insight into the kind of acceptance Jesus offered people. Read John 1:35-51. Look at His personal style in talking to Andrew, Simon, Philip, and Nathaniel. What kind of people were each of these, and what kind of acceptance did Jesus offer?

MIGHT: In a group, try to list a number of traits and practices that people in your church use to give or deny acceptance. Try to pinpoint specifically what kinds of people you tend to reject. Analyze why you do that. Come up with several steps you can take to rid yourselves of that perspective.

TUESDAY: Let me be who I am!

HEART: Ever just wish people would accept you for you? Not your abilities. Not what you can do for the team. Or how you always give of yourself. Or the fact that you're good at drawing. But you. Just you. Everything about you—your foibles, your bigger than average nose, your clumsiness.

You know what it is to feel rejected, don't you?

People looking your way, then talking secretly and laughing.

Being the last one chosen for the team.

Having no one to dance with.

Hearing someone groan when it's your turn to recite.

Sitting alone on the bus.

Finding a nasty note taped to your locker.

Running for office and getting only one vote—yours.

It only takes one. One rotten person. And you can be wiped out for weeks!

There's a story about a soldier who arrived home on leave in the middle of World War II. He disembarked in New York City and called his folks. Everyone was overjoyed when he phoned and made plans to meet him at the train station. But then the GI stammered, "Mom, Dad, I have a friend with me. I wonder if you might put him up during my leave. But he has some problems: he's partially blind, and he has a leg shot off. Would you mind?"

The mother sighed. "Well, bring him home, honey, but we wouldn't want him to stay more than a day or two."

The GI sadly hung up the phone. Sometime later they found his body in a hotel room, dead. He only had one leg, and they said he was almost blind.

Those parents wept for their loss. But more than that, they wept for a guilt they could probably never forgive themselves for.

SOUL: Alain, a French philosopher and essayist, wrote, "It's a small thing to accept people for what they are; if we really love them we must want them to be what they are."

When it comes to those God-given traits which no one but God can change—looks, race, personality, talents, abilities—Christians offer total acceptance. On the other hand, when it comes to things like sinful actions and words, we seek to love the sinner but not the sin.

Real acceptance doesn't mean toleration of evil. Rather, it says, "I will love you despite your evil, and will even help you to shed your evil. But even if you don't turn from your evil, I will still love you."

MIND: Remember the scene in John 13 where Jesus washed the disciples' feet? Read through the passage (John 13:1-30). Notice two things: where Judas Iscariot is first mentioned and when he leaves the upper room. After you read answer this question: Did Jesus wash his feet, too?

MIGHT: Think about a person in your group whom you find very hard to accept or even like. Try to pinpoint what it is about him or her that makes this so hard. Determine whether your reasons are because of sin on their part, or because of certain quirks of their personality that God has given them which you simply don't like. Then read Colossians 3:12. How can you put on the kind of heart towards them that Paul writes about? List several ways, pick one out and try it.

WEDNESDAY: The ugliness of prejudice

HEART: In the 1960s racial prejudice and anger flamed as blacks, under the leadership of Martin Luther King, Jr. and Ralph Abernathy, sought to knock down the walls cutting them off from the mainstream. It was in this context that a young mother sent her first-grade daughter off to her newly integrated school. The mother was nervous about it, and when her daughter returned she asked how things had gone.

"Oh, mother! You know what? A little Negro girl sat down next to me!" the youngster exclaimed.

Hoping for the best but full of fear about what thoughts this might have provoked, Mom asked, "And what happened?"

The child explained, "We were both so scared that we held hands all day long."

Perhaps that's what we really need—enough of a scare that we realize how much we need one another!

SOUL: One way Paul pictured the body of Christ was as a mixture of many people—from every background and race. Paul wrote to the Colossians that we're not to lie to one another because we've put on the "new self," a self that is being renewed every day. He says it's a renewal in which "there is no Greek or Jew, circumcised or uncircumcised, barbarian, Scythian, slave or free"(Colossians 3:11).

It's difficult for most of us to visualize what a monumental statement this was in Paul's day. Fierce prejudices raged among people back then, much like today. Jews regarded all non-Jews—Gentiles—as "dogs" and called them that to their faces. Samaritans were half-breeds. On the other hand, Romans looked upon Jews with complete contempt. The name most of us go by—"Christians"—was originally offered as a mocking nickname for followers of Christ—"little Christs."

In our day, there are a multitude of epithets we use for people of other races and nationalities. What might surprise you is that people of other nations often regard Americans and "whites" with similar derision. In India, if your shadow so much as falls on a devout Hindu, he must wash that "defilement" off by dipping himself in the Ganges River. Black Africans, when they first encountered "white men," felt sorry for them because their skin had no color. They thought these people were ghosts. Eskimoes call a person who is a lazy, useless good-for-nothing and a constant irritation a "white man"!

Christ came to free us from the chains of mental and emotional prejudice. Paul's words to the Ephesians illuminate the point: "For he himself is our peace, who has made the two one and has destroyed the barrier, the dividing wall of hostility, by abolishing in his flesh the law. . . Consequently, you are no longer foreigners and aliens, but fellow citizens with God's people, and members of God's household"(Ephesians 2:14-15,19).

Think of it—in Christ we are all citizens of the new kingdom, brothers and sisters, a family. There is no more reason to draw lines or make distinctions. We are one.

MIND: Read what Paul told the Ephesians on the subject of acceptance based on the final destruction of prejudice. You'll find his words in Ephesians 2:11-22 and 3:1-13.

MIGHT: Take a look at your own prejudices. We all have them. What matters is how we deal with them. What insight does Paul provide from the passages in Ephesians?

THURSDAY: The speck and the stick

HEART: Anyone who thinks Jesus was a humorless moralist hasn't reckoned with His marvelous wit as it often came out in His illustrations. One example occurs in Matthew 7:1-4 where Jesus addresses the issue of judging one another. He asks, "Why do you look at the speck of sawdust in your brother's eye and pay no attention to the plank in your own eye?"

A speck. That's tiny. A dot. But in your eye, it can become terrifically irritating.

But a plank? A log? A two by four? In your eye? Can you see a guy walking along with one of those monsters sticking out at everyone? Every time he turns around, he takes out about 20 people. You have one of those things in your eye and you've got serious problems.

But what's even more remarkable is that this fellow with the two-by-four scurries around inspecting everyone else. He's got a magnifying glass and when he spots a speck, boy does he raise a ruckus. "Hey, hey, what have we here? Come look everybody—a speck in the eye. Man, you must be an awful person to be going around with a speck like that."

Meanwhile, his own plank is dangling right in your face. How can you not help but laugh?

SOUL: It's true. That's what it's like to be judgmental. Always going around looking for specks in others when your own problem is so obvious.

How can you tell if you're judgmentai? Take a little test.

1. What do you most notice about the people around you—what they do right, or what they do wrong?
2. What do you take most pleasure in—finding someone doing something right, or finding someone doing something wrong?
3. What do you tell other people about—what you saw so and so doing right, or what you saw him doing wrong?

4. How do you measure yourself against others—
    by how many things they do right which you do
    better, or by how many things they do wrong
    which you don't do at all (or think you don't do
    at all)?

Take inventory. If you're the type who's always
noticing the wrong in others and secretly gloating
about it, you're judgmental.

That's not what we strive for in the body of Christ.
Acceptance, love, compasssion and kindness are our
trade vocabulary.

MIND: Read Matthew 7:1-5 and John 7:24. What is
the difference between judging "by mere appear-
ances" and making "a right judgment"? Does Jesus'
statement in Matthew 7 mean we're never to notice
or point out the sins of others?

MIGHT: A high school girl developed a crush on her
English teacher. Finally, she wrote him a love letter.
The letter came back without a caring comment—and
it was edited and red-penciled where she'd made
grammatical and punctuational errors!

What might you have to say to such an attitude?
How would you have handled such a problem? How
can you help other Christians around you to be more
accepting and less judgmental?

FRIDAY: Teacher's pet

HEART: Fortunately (or unfortunately, as the case

may be), I was never any "teacher's pet." I had one French prof who nicknamed me "Littlecrunch" and repeatedly humiliated me in class, but that was the closest I ever came. I don't know whether he simply liked to pick on people like me, or whether this was some sadistic way of showing he liked me. Whichever it was, it wasn't pleasant.

Still, I remember one fellow in school who became the classic teacher's pet. It was in art class. The fellow—his name was Joe—I have to admit, was brilliant. He could draw anything, and what he drew looked like the thing he was drawing. It was not only recognizable, it was better!

This particular teacher held Joe up as the last, greatest and final hope of mankind. I don't know how that fit into an art class in a huge New Jersey high school, but that's the impression I had.

When you needed an idea, the answer was "Joe, help this guy out."

When you finally turned in a project, it was always exhibited as a contrast to Joe's perfect rendition.

When the contest was over and Joe had won, the whole wall was devoted to his year's work.

Yuck. I still don't like the guy.

SOUL: What is such behavior? Favoritism. James punched the lights out on that issue in the first century. He wrote, "My brothers, as believers in our glorious Lord Jesus Christ, don't show favoritism. Suppose a man comes into your meeting wearing a gold ring and fine clothes, and a poor man in shabby clothes also comes in. If you show special attention to the man wearing fine clothes and say, 'Here's a good seat for you,' but say to the poor man, 'You stand there' or 'Sit on the floor by my feet,' have you not discriminated among yourselves and become judges with evil thoughts?" (James 2:1-3).

Indeed, favoritism—the kind that picks the rich over the poor, the popular over the nerdy, the smart over the dumb—has existed since people have had eyesight.

MIND: You'll read about another brand of favoritism in Luke 7:36-50. Do you ever find yourself rejecting people because of their "reputation"?

MIGHT: When you sit down at the lunch table today, take a moment and think if you notice anyone who's on the "outs" trying to get on the "in"? What can you say or do to encourage them?

On the other hand, what if you're that person on the outside looking in? What steps can you take to try to bridge that gap?

SATURDAY/SUNDAY: Reach out and touch some heart

HEART:
It's a coldness
That you can't escape
No matter how hot the bath water is.
It's a dampness
You try to evaporate
By walking in the sun,

But somehow it clings damper
In the unfriendly sneer of a stranger.

It's an ache
Deep down in the bones
That you try to cover
With smiles and laughs
But they're all sucked hollow.

It's a waiting,
An always waiting
For the next thing,
The next someone.
Maybe they'll understand.
Maybe they'll listen.
Maybe they'll be your friend.

SOUL: Loneliness. How do you break the cold, the damp, the ache, the waiting?

I'm convinced loneliness is much more than being alone. It's a feeling inside that no one knows you, no one understands what goes on inside your heart, what thoughts clang around inside your soul. It's feeling you can't tell anyone who you really are, because if you do and they don't like it, what else do you have?

Acceptance is something you get; it's also something you give. You reach out. You try to make contact. You touch. Maybe there's a spark. Maybe there's a jolt. Maybe there's nothing.

But at least you tried.

MIND: There's a story I've always loved. You'll find it in Matthew 8:1-4. Read it now, paying particular attention to how the leper approached Jesus and how Jesus responded.

MIGHT: Did you note that Jesus "reached out his hand and touched him." Only a leper could fully appreciate such a simple gesture. Lepers had to cry out to everyone who came near, "Unclean! Unclean!" If you touched a leper in Jesus' day, you also became unclean. How do you think a leper might have felt under those conditions? How do you think this leper might have reacted when Jesus touched him? Is there someone you know who is, in a sense, regarded as a leper? What can you do to show him or her acceptance in Christ?

3

Put Her First? You've Got to Be Kidding!

Honor one another above yourselves.

Romans 12:10

MONDAY: "I don't get no respect!"

HEART: Two events from my high school days have seared themselves into my memory. One happened to me; the other happened through me. Let me tell you about the second first.

The president of our student council in high school was fairly typical. Political. Popular. Ambitious. Hard-driving. Not a jock. Somewhat intellectual. His name was Ira. But he had one major problem. Like Rodney Dangerfield, he didn't get no respect. A little here and there. A rah now and then. But when he gave speeches, we snored. When he roused us up, we doused him down.

His worst moment happened one Friday afternoon after school hours. About seven of us decided an "elimination" was in order. We armed ourselves with water derringers, water machine guns, water rifles and balloon-bombs. I crept down the hall towards the office, then waved my comrades on. In a few moments it was over. Ira's psyche lay splattered in a pool of water, his self-image permanently drowned in a splish of spray. As we careened back out and down the hall, the student council teacher advisor ran out after us, swearing and sermonizing. But our glee only echoed louder through the corridors. We had water-assassinated our student body president.

The other example knocked me personally. For four months my girlfriend had to drive the car on dates. I was younger than her and didn't have a license. But the day came for me to take my driver's test. In only a few hours I'd become a card-carrying expediter of the expressway.

But I flunked the test!

I flunked! Even my mother cried.

That was tough enough. I came to school, my girlfriend rushed out to greet me, and I gave her the sad news. Unfortunately, I also told my assassination-plot friends. The next day, I discovered they'd taken control of the copy room and taped signs all over the high school byways and boardrooms, reading: "Mark Littleton—Driver of the Year!"

Now that's lack of respect, friend.

SOUL: Oh, how we love the limelight! But sometimes the limelight becomes the lemonlight, doesn't it? Especially when the cameras focus on us in a humbling moment.

But respect is what Romans 12:10 is all about.

Read the verse: "Honor one another above your-selves." Some scholars translate it, "Outdo one another in showing respect." But another way of looking at it speaks of how we treat one another—with honor, deference, consideration. Are you considerate of others' feelings, needs, concerns, hopes, fears? Are you courteous around people? Do you have good manners?

That's part of it. But it's much more. Respect is to "consider someone worthy of high regard," as Webster's dictionary puts it. Notice that the burden is not on the one respected. That is, we don't give them respect because they deserve it. Rather, we respect them because it's right to respect beings made in the image of God, even if they don't deserve it. As they say in the Army, "If you can't salute the man, salute the uniform." In other words, "If you can't respect him for his person, at least respect him because God made him."

MIND: Take a little trip today through three verses on respect and honor: John 4:44, Ephesians 6:2 and First Peter 3:17. What do you see in these examples about honor, who gets it and why they should get it?

MIGHT: We speak of respect as being something a person earns. Come up with three reasons why respect should be given even if it isn't earned. Now ask your parents if you have been showing them respect, and if not, how you can improve.

TUESDAY: Reverence

HEART:
Sometimes you see it in the way Grandma looks at Grandpa
and how she listens when he speaks.

Sometimes you see it when the President walks
into the East Room, and the reporters hush
before he speaks.

You might recognize it in a dog's eyes
as he waits for the command
that will bring him a bone.

Or perhaps you'll spot it at a party,
the way a guy opens the door for a girl,
and doesn't even pretend embarrassment.

But mostly, mostly,
you'll catch it only briefly
in the glint of an eye,
in the slight turn of a head,
in the bending of an ear downward
only briefly.
It's worth gold
to the heart of the one who receives it.

SOUL: Reverence. It's part of the Scout Law. "A Scout is trustworthy, loyal, helpful, . . . brave, clean, and reverent."

It always kind of startled me, the way it was stuck

on at the end of 12 majestic terms. It seemed foreign.

Until I became a Christian.

I think to some degree only the Christian can truly understand reverence. It's a holy term. One we use in reference to God, church, worship, those things. But it's also the way we're supposed to treat one another. With reverence.

How on earth do you do that? I mean, Joe? Bill? Harry? Chuck? Jill? Gwenn?

Come on. They're all part of the gang. I don't need to "reverence" them.

Oh? Read Romans 12:10 again: "Honor one another above yourselves." That word for honor brings with it the idea of reverence. It's more than respect. Ever hear the expression, "A reverence for life"? That's when people have such a deep respect and concern for life that they'll never do anything to mar, mutilate or maim it.

Think about it. That's how God says we're to treat others, especially our brothers and sisters in Christ.

MIND: To get a clearer idea of what reverence is, read Isaiah 6. How did Isaiah feel in the presence of God?

MIGHT: Reverence doesn't mean trembling with fear in the presence of one another, but there is a sense in which we're to so reverence one another that we seek nothing but what is best and good for them.

How's your reverence quotient? Do you have a

sense of awe in the fact that you see, hear and enjoy one another? Do you experience that exuberance in fellowship that comes from true respect and care—the same kind you'd feel in the presence of a king, or queen or president?

WEDNESDAY: The killer

HEART: "I think the guy's a complete jerk," Matt said.

Bob looked up. "How come? He seems all right to me."

"Oh, retch me one. Just cause he's on the basketball team at CHS, people think he's the last great hope. And the way he's always answering questions in class. Like he's the walking Bible or something. It makes me sick." Matt's face wrinkled with disgust.

Bob snickered. "You sound like you're a little jealous of him."

Matt's face immediately turned dark. His eyes flashed. "Don't give me that. There's nothing to be jealous of. The guy's just a jerk."

"Then why are you always talking about him? You talk about him more than any person in the whole class, even Wendy."

Matt sighed. "Get off it. I'm not always talking about him. That's ridiculous."

"You are. Last week. Two weeks ago. Why a month ago you were so heated up I thought you wanted to punch him out."

Matt looked away. He wondered about it. He knew

the truth. Bob was right. He was jealous, but he couldn't admit that.

SOUL: Jealousy can eat you up. It's one of those emotions we often don't understand in ourselves. We ask, "Why do I feel this way? Why can't I let it go?" But it hangs on like rust on chrome.

Do you ever get jealous of others?

The guy whom all the girls swoon over?

The jock who takes away all the awards?

The cheerleader who never seems to get a blemish on her cheeks or a run in her stockings?

The math/physics/chemistry/English/etc. whiz who aces all the tests?

Jealousy can strike at the oddest moments. Like a hornet's nest, it seems to buzz inside you. Every time you look at the person you feel a mixture of anger, resentment and bitterness.

MIND: You're not alone. Several people in Scripture had the same problem. Read first about Saul in First Samuel 18:6-16. Then look at Cain and Abel in Genesis 4:1-8. Finally, read what jealousy does in the church body in James 3:13-18.

MIGHT: Jealousy kills fellowship among Christians. It turns us from comrades into competitors, from encouragers into enemies. Take a close look at your thoughts today. See if you can spot a few that clang with the death knell of jealousy. When you catch one, ask yourself why you feel that way. Then stop and pray that God would bless the person you're jealous of. It may release you from that prison of pain that jealousy creates.

THURSDAY: Self-exaltation

HEART: There's an old joke about four people on a small airplane flying over Kansas. One's the President of the U.S., Richard Nixon; the second is his Secretary of State, Henry Kissinger, sometimes known as "the smartest man in the world"; the third's Billy Graham; and the fourth's a hippie with a beard, long hair and a knapsack. Suddenly the captain comes on the intercom and says, "Mayday! Mayday! We're going to crash. There are parachutes under your seats. I'm going to jump." A second later, he's gone.

Frantically, the four passengers check the seats. They discover there are only threee parachutes. Everyone looks at everyone else wondering who will stay. Nixon speaks first. "Gentlemen, I'm the President of the U.S. I can't die. I'll take the first parachute." He takes one and jumps.

Kissinger is next. "Gentlemen, the world can't afford to lose me. I'm the smartest man in the world. I'll take the second parachute." He jumps.

Billy Graham looks at the hippie and says, "Son, you take the last parachute. I've lived my life. And I'll just go to be with the Lord anyway. So go ahead. Don't mind me."

But suddenly the hippie says, "Hey, Billy, no sweat. There are two parachutes left. You take one and I'll take the other."

"But how?" asks Billy. "I thought there were only three."

"Well, see," says the hippie, "the smartest man in the world just jumped out with my knapsack on his back!"

SOUL: That's meant to get at least a snicker, so snicker anyway.

But there is a point. It takes some kind of ego to start thinking of yourself as the smartest man in the world, doesn't it? Such thinking might be labeled pride, or self-centeredness, or plain egotistical nonsense. But those who do it take it most seriously. The Bible calls it self-exaltation. Many of us practice such thinking without even realizing it.

How? Just consider how many times you tell yourself things like . . .

You know, you're a lot smarter than the teachers give you credit for, Jones.

You would have caught that pass easy, Smith, if TJ had thrown it properly.

You should have won, Boyle. The judges were just stupid.

If I ever really studied, man, I'd get straight A's too.

People talk plenty about "poor self-image" and "low self-esteem." But if we're honest with ourselves, we soon admit that we have a lot of pride, too. Some of our thoughts are downright egotistical!

Face it. We all have that problem. It's another of those internal habits that keeps us from truly accepting one another. We're so concerned about me, myself and I that we forget him, herself and them.

MIND: Read Philippians 2:3-4 for some insight into how God wants us to operate in relation to others.

MIGHT: Do you ever find yourself thinking proud, egotistical thoughts? Take a moment to reflect on it. Notice in particular how those thoughts make you feel about others and what you say and do to them. Pick someone out in your class who appears to have a measure of true humility. See if you can spend a little time with them. Notice how they talk, what they say. How much of it is directed to others? How much demonstrates true acceptance?

FRIDAY: Putting others ahead of yourself

HEART: Whenever some extra pie or cake was left after a meal, my brother, sister and I used to engage in lengthy discussions about precisely how such remnants ought to be divided. I was the eldest, I argued, so I ought to get the supreme cut.

Usually my sister opted out in the name of female beauty and a desire to stay the right weight. So it was me against my younger brother.

If Mom tried to divide the cake, there was an instant argument.

I'd say, "I get first pick."

Steve would lament, "His piece is bigger than mine."

Mom would switch pieces.

"Unfair! Unfair! I wanted that piece."

To resolve such difficulties my Dad had a trick. Or, should I say, an equalizer. "One cuts, the other chooses."

Why do parents have to come up with these things?

Believe me, whoever did the cutting got out a micrometer. You couldn't tell those two pieces apart if you did a genetic study on them!

SOUL: Just the same, what if my bro and I had taken another course? What if we consciously decided to put the other first—like cut the cake and then offer the larger piece to the other anyway? (Of course, then you could get into an argument about who's going to be the humbler of the two. But that's TRULY rare.)

Honoring one another involves putting the other first. Did you ever hear the little slogan—"J-O-Y—Jesus first; others second; you last"? Hard to do, isn't it? Well nigh improbable for most of us.

But not impossible.

Selfishness is deep. But Christ is deeper, and He can do excavation work on even those of us most full of ourselves.

MIND: Read Philippians 2:5-8 for some insight into how Jesus put others before Himself.

MIGHT: Keep a little diary for a week. Write down each day one selfish act you committed, and one selfless deed you did for another. At the end of the week, review. How did you feel about all those acts of selfishness? What about the acts of giving? Which is better? Why?

SATURDAY/SUNDAY:
God honors us, too!

HEART: What's your favorite passage of Scripture? If you're like me, you're always finding new ones. A recent find of mine comes out of Revelation 3:5: "He who overcomes will, like them, be dressed in white. I will never blot out his name from the book of life, but will acknowledge his name before my Father and his angels." What strikes me is the statement, "I will acknowledge his name before my Father . . . etc." What does it mean that Jesus will acknowledge us before the Father?

Remember when you were in elementary school at recess and the Phys. Ed. director had two kids choose up teams? Were you ever the LAST ONE chosen? Ugh! ("No, not me . . . Uh-uh.") Well I remember being the last guy a few times! Remember how you felt as things wound down and you still weren't chosen? Maybe you ended up being the last one. (Maybe there was even an argument about who had to take you!) Wasn't something inside of you pleading, "Please don't let me be last. Please choose me. Please, this time." You look at the choosers with pleading eyes. Wasn't your heart pounding, just a little?

All of us have been in that position sometime,

because no one is best at everything. Well, imagine you're in heaven and it's time for Jesus and Satan to choose up teams. Those who go with Jesus go to heaven. And those with Satan go—well, you know.

What do you think might be happening as the two selectors go through the process? A drumming heart? Sweaty palms? Dry mouth?

But what if Jesus stood up, and immediately He looked at you and said, "Come on; you're on My team"?

SOUL: That, in a sense, is a small part of what it means that Jesus will "acknowledge" us before the Father and the angels. He'll proclaim we're "on His team" without a hint of reservation or hesitation. He's proud to make it known!

Isn't that idea thrilling? Jesus will honor us in the presence of all heaven and earth and declare, "He's with Me. He's on My team. He's one of My family."

Isn't that the essence of honoring another—being willing to stand up with a brother or sister in Christ and say, "I'm with them. We're in this together"?

Take a little test:

Do you ever shrink from identifying with someone from your Sunday School group while you're on the secular school grounds?

Do you ever pretend you don't know someone who is regarded by the others as a bit different, uncool or rejected?

Do you ever wish someone from church wouldn't hang around you the way they do on non-church time?

MIND: How'd you do? Read Romans 12:10 again and list three ways you can apply it today now that you've come to the end of the week.

MIGHT: Here's a quote from the Lord you might want to memorize: "Those who honor me, I will honor" (1 Samuel 2:30). Perhaps you can turn that Scripture around and apply it to His people, too.

4

Hey, I Don't Tell Anyone What I Do Wrong

Therefore, confess your sins to one another, and pray for one another so that you may be healed; the effective prayer of a righteous man can accomplish much.

James 5:16, NASB

MONDAY: One of the hardest things in the world

HEART: The sheriff heard shooting in the saloon and skedaddled over to find two men at the point of killing one another. "What's this all about?" shouted the grim sheriff, parting the two cowboys.

"He called me a liar!" the first shouted.

"Well, he is!" retorted the other. "He lies all the time to everyone and this time he lied to me!"

The sheriff squinted at the accused. "Is this true?"

"What if it is?" roared the cowpoke. "I have a right to be sensitive about it, don't I?"

Ah, the truth. Hurts. A lot.

"One of the hardest things in the world to do is to admit you are wrong. And nothing is more helpful in resolving a situation than its frank admission."

47

That cowboy, numerous Christians and those involved in recent scandals in the United States might have taken those words to heart. They were spoken by Benjamin Disraeli, Prime Minister of Great Britain in the late 1800s.

Few of us take such ideas seriously. We simply don't want to admit we're wrong, that we've sinned, that we've made a mess of things. But it's the first important step on the road to recovery—and forgiveness.

SOUL: Confession of sin ranks high among those who seek to build solid, lasting relationships for the kingdom of God. But what is it to "confess your sins to one another," as James says?

The word used by James literally means to "speak the same thing," to agree, admit, come to terms. The idea is that God confronts you with the truth, and you agree that it's the truth. You say the same thing about it. "You told a lie." "Yes, I told a lie."

Still, confession is more than just admitting the truth. There's an element in it which also says, "I don't want to continue doing this evil. I want to change."

Even Christians find confession of sin difficult. It's one thing to kneel down by your bed and tell the Lord about all your shortcomings. It's quite another to say those things in front of several friends, churchgoers and neighbors. The embarrassment quotient goes way up. But at the same time, your stature and humility before others can increase, too.

MIND: Read about David's confession of sin in Psalm 51 after his adultery with Bathsheba. What elements of it stand out to you? How does the whole situation strike you? Is David's honesty attractive or repulsive?

MIGHT: Ask yourself who among your closest Christian friends could you confess a besetting sin to—a sin that troubles you and which you've been unable to overcome? Start building a closer relationship with several in your group whom you might pray for and tell about your problems and needs. The point of confession of sin is not just to "get it off your chest," but to enlist the help, prayers and love of others to defeat the fault.

TUESDAY: Who and how many?

HEART: A man stood in a large congregation. That evening the church featured a sharing service where members took the opportunity to make prayer requests, ask for songs and share testimonies. The man felt nervous and upset. But he felt he had to say what was on his heart.

The church was quiet. He finally had his chance to speak. "For many years now I have had a severe problem in my home. No one outside has known about it. But my wife, my children and I need your help. We ask for your prayers. The problem . . . "

He paused. It was as though something inside him was twisting and wrenching.

Finally, he said, "My problem is child abuse. I

have abused my daughter for nearly five years."

His voice cracked. As he sat down, he murmured, "I desperately need your help."

An embarrassed silence hung over the church from the back pew to the pulpit. Finally, the elder leading the service cleared his throat and said, "Would someone pray for this brother?"

Another man rose and began praying.

SOUL: Such a confession contains much of the drama of a Hollywood spectacle. A public cleansing like that detonates like a nuclear explosion—even if the result is an anxious silence. People often don't know how to take it or deal with it. Afterwards they may make a special effort to avoid this man, so terrible was his sin.

Is this the kind of thing James meant we should do—stand up in front of the whole church and unbare our deepest secrets?

I think not. James said, "Confess your sins to one another." That "one another" can mean anywhere from one to one thousand. But more likely, it's reserved for only a few.

Some Christians make much of the need for giant public confessions of sin in order for things to be forgiven and cleansed. But the Bible never calls for such mortifying acts. Confession to one or two is usually enough. Many people aren't prepared to deal with or live with the sins of others. Such public cleansings can actually do more harm than good.

If you're thinking about the need to confess your sins, remember several points:

1. Reveal them only to people who can help, pray
   and keep quiet.
2. Don't use it as a public platform to whip yourself.
3. Your purpose is to be healed, not martyred.
4. Private sins call for private confessions.

The only time a public confession is required is
when the person involved is a public personality
whose sin has had a public effect.

MIND: Notice again how David handled the confrontation and confession that followed his sin with
Bathsheba (see 2 Samuel 12:13-23). What principles
can you apply from this text to your situation?

MIGHT: Sometimes Christians use public forums
to confess their sins almost as a chance to demon-
strate how awful they were. Occasionally people
take pleasure in telling others their sins because it
makes them somehow appear to be "with it" or
"cool," not a "goody-goody." Examine yourself and
think through the reasons you would tell someone
about a sin you have. Determine to use this element
of Christian life as a means to heal, not harm.

WEDNESDAY: Activate the memory

HEART: Frequently the biggest problem with confession of sin is beginning. "Where do I start?" we
ask. If you'll follow my lead in the paragraphs ahead,
you may be in for one of the most freeing and uplifting experiences of your life. And convicting.

Dr. Joe Aldrich has written an excellent book called *Inner Beauty*. In it he discusses confession of sin. The beginning point, he suggests, is "activating your memory." Ask the Holy Spirit to guide your thoughts as you ask yourself these questions:

1. *To whom have I lied?*
2. *From whom have I stolen?*
3. *Who has been a victim of my temper?*
4. *Toward whom am I bitter, refusing to forgive?*
5. *Against whose authority have I rebelled?*
6. *Whose reputation have I damaged by slander or gossip?*

At first you may try to "block" your mental images as the Spirit speaks to your heart. But resist the ploys of Satan. Let the Spirit speak—clearly and directly.

SOUL: This can be a soul-wrenching experience. Even as I did it myself I found myself afraid to go on from question to question, fearful something would come to mind that I wouldn't want to deal with. Are you in that struggle now? If so, stop, pray, ask the Lord for courage and the fortitude to press on. Believe me, Satan will do anything to keep you from following through on this.

MIND: Read Daniel's prayer in Daniel 9:3-19 for insight into the process of prayer and confession together.

MIGHT: How are you doing? Wrung out? Weary? Argumentative? Coming up with rationalizations for all those sins? It's a battle. But hang tough. The worst isn't over yet.

THURSDAY: Plan your script

HEART: A little girl barged into the kitchen breathless with a wild story. "Mommy, there was a lion in the park!"

"A lion!" her mother answered. "Come now. Are you sure it wasn't a dog or a kitty cat? This isn't another story, is it?"

The little girl stomped her foot. "Mommy, it was a lion, a big yellow one."

That night Mom decided she'd better have a talk with her daughter. She suggested the little girl needed to confess her fib to the Lord and ask His forgiveness. Penitent, the little girl went upstairs and knelt by her bed. A few minutes later she came back downstairs.

"Well, did you ask the Lord for forgiveness, honey?"

"Yes, Mother," the child replied. "I did ask Him, but He said, 'Don't mention it, Miss Mary; that big yellow dog has often fooled Me, too.'"

A cute story, but we do like to make up stories and good excuses about our sins, don't we? Still, it's wise to take inventory and deal with real sins each day. Sir William Osler, a famous English scientist and a Christian, once said, "Undress your soul at night, not by self-examination, but by shedding as you do your garments, the daily sins whether of omission or commission, and you will wake a free man, with a new life."

I'd have to disagree a bit that self-examination isn't part of the process; it is. But Osler has a point.

How then do you go about this? Ask yourself the questions listed yesterday and write down your answers. Then confess them to the Lord first. If necessary, you may need to go to an injured party and ask forgiveness. Sometimes restitution—a payment back of money, service or something else—is also necessary to right the wrong. Only you can decide what should be done. Right now, ask the Lord to open your mind and reveal to you any sins you need to be cleansed of. Write them down. Don't be afraid. The Lord will not be hard on you. But this process is essential for real freedom.

SOUL: Now that you've made it this far, think through whom you should go to. In some cases you may not need to talk directly to anyone. The sin is a secret one, between you and God. He forgives. Accept His forgiveness. You have to make a choice: Is it necessary for my "victim" to know that I did this? Will his knowing make matters worse? There are many times that secret sins should remain a secret only God knows about. Why should you put your garbage in my yard so I have to smell it and scrutinize it?

On the other hand, your sin may be "secret" in that the victim knows nothing about it. But it was something beyond simple internal bitterness or anger.

Perhaps you stole something, or told a lie or gossiped to someone in a nasty fashion. Even though the "sinnee" may not know about it, in some cases you may need to confess your sin verbally to them. To decide, seek out the counsel of someone you trust.

Still, there are some sins you know you need to discuss with your victim(s). They know about it and so do you. You have to swab the deck together. In such a case, prepare carefully what you want to say. Give them a clear and direct description of the trespass. Don't hedge or play anything down. Then tell them you're sorry and ask their forgiveness: "Will you forgive me?"

MIND: Boy, I'm sweating just writing this. It's tough, isn't it? But it's the only way to freedom from guilt. Read about two contrasting reactions to similar sins on the part of Peter (Luke 22:54-62) and Judas Iscariot (Matthew 27:3-10).

MIGHT: You're probably saying at this point, "Why are you doing this to me?"

I'm not. We all do it to ourselves by sinning in the first place. My hope is that you will take this lesson seriously and make a practice of righting the wrongs you commit. Remember Proverbs 28:13: "He who conceals his sins does not prosper; but whoever confesses and renounces them finds mercy."

FRIDAY: Expect a battle

HEART: Dr. Harry Ironside once wrote about a young

boatbuilder who listened to a sermon on confession of sin. The man was greatly convicted and came up afterwards for counsel. He told the pastor he had a genuine dilemma. He was employed by an unbeliever to whom he'd often witnessed about Jesus. But the man only scoffed and ridiculed him.

In the meantime, the Christian had been building a boat in his own back yard and stealing copper nails from his employer to use for the construction. He said to the pastor, "I'm guilty of something that, if I should acknowledge it to my employer, it would ruin my testimony forever." For some time he'd rationalized his sin, telling himself his employer would never miss the nails. But he knew something had to be done.

In the end, he decided to pay for the nails and confess his sin.

"And what did the man say when you told him?" asked his pastor.

"Oh, he looked queerly at me, then exclaimed, 'George, I always did think you were just a hypocrite, but now I begin to feel there's something in this Christianity after all. Any religion that would make a dishonest workman come back and confess that he had been stealing copper nails and offer to settle for them must be worth having.'"

SOUL: Like the boatbuilder, you'll probably face a battle when you decide to confess any sins you may have to others. What kind of battle?

Dr. Joe Aldrich suggests several lines of sinful logic:

   • "Things have improved." Perhaps, but the point

is that the Christian needs a clear conscience, not just peaceful relations.

• "It happened years ago; why dredge up the past?" But you do remember it, don't you? And it irks your soul—right? Then you're not dredging up anything—the Spirit is reminding you to get it right.

• "It's such an insignificant offense." Hmmm. Not bad reasoning. But if it's been weighing on your conscience, that's significant enough.

• "Everyone makes mistakes." Absolutely. That's why you need to correct yours.

• "It will only make matters worse." The point is, are you willing to obey God now in this situation? Don't worry about making matters worse. Leave that in God's hands. You do what's right now.

MIND: Look at the story of Zaccheus in Luke 19:1-10. What was he willing to do for anyone he'd wronged?

MIGHT: This has been a tough lesson. It's getting tougher all the time. But already I've seen some important changes in my life. Are you seeing them in yours?

SATURDAY/SUNDAY:
Worthwhile rewards

HEART: When I first began meditating on this issue, I was deeply convicted. I realized I had to do the thing I was exhorting you to do. As a result, I found myself confessing several sins to people—one to my boss, several to my wife, another to my daughter, and another to an editor I work with. Each time there was an inner fight. But in each case, I received forgiveness and a new sense of freedom and joy in the relationship. Suddenly the barriers fell down. I felt renewed, enlarged, hopeful about the future. There's a cleanness about forgiveness that is beautiful. Do you sense it?

SOUL:
I remember that snow storm.
Deep white.
Tracks—precise, clean, etched.
On your tongue, a sparkly crunch.
Water—cold, rippling down the throat.

Then there was the snow
by the road.
Cakey black.
Streaks of cinder.
Ugly.
Pure white with cinder smoke
is unequalled ugliness.

Oh God, let me be pure white inside.
Wash away the gray
and the black.
Let me be new.
Today.
This moment.
And forever.

MIND: Read a famous verse in Isaiah 1:18. "You shall be white as . . . "

MIGHT: One more thing about confession of sin. I'll frame it in an old story. Three chaplains were on the front during World War II. As they neared the place where the enemy fired on their men, they thought it would be wise to confess their sins to one another. The Catholic chaplain said, "Well, men, I suppose I'll be the first, being Catholic and all. Men, I have to admit, I have an impulse to drink too much now and then. I fight it, but I fall, too."

The Protestant chaplain nodded and said, "Well, I don't have a taste for liquor, but my problem concerns the ladies. I fight it desperately, but every now and then I'm tempted and I fall."

There was a long pause and all eyes fell on the Jewish chaplain. One of the others said, "And you, Chaplain Cohen, do you have a besetting sin?"

The Jewish chaplain sighed and said, "I'm afraid so. I have this terrible, irresistible impulse to gossip—and I can't wait to get to a phone!"

One thing about confession of sin—once confessed and forgiven, it goes no further. Not a millimeter. Right?

5

What Do You Think I Am—Your Personal Servant?

Whoever wants to become great among you must be your servant, and whoever wants to be first must be your slave—just as the Son of Man did not come to be served, but to serve, and to give His life as a ransom for many.

Matthew 20:26-28

MONDAY: It was a dark and stormy night . . .

HEART: Many years ago, an elderly man and his wife entered a small hotel in Philadelphia. A storm raged outside. The man told the clerk all the large hotels in town were filled. "Could you possibly give us a room here?"

The clerk informed the traveler the town was teeming with conventions. No rooms anywhere. "Still, I can't send a nice couple like you out in the rain," he said. "Would you perhaps be willing to sleep in my room?"

The couple said they couldn't take his room, but

the clerk insisted. They accepted. The next morning while paying their bill the man said, "You ought to be the boss of the best hotel in the United States. Maybe someday I'll build one for you."

Everyone laughed. But two years later the clerk received a letter from the man, inviting him to New York. A round trip ticket was enclosed.

When he arrived, the man drove him to a huge new building on Fifth Avenue. He said, "This is the hotel I've just built for you to manage."

The clerk was astonished. "Who are you?"

"My name is William Waldorf Astor." And this was the birth of the original Waldorf-Astoria Hotel. George Boldt became its first manager.

SOUL: There's another story about a hotel in the Bible that you know well. It's the story of the birth of Jesus. And for Him there was no room at the inn either. If He came to your door on a dark and stormy night, would you let Him in? Would you offer Him your bed?

Being a servant doesn't just count in the big moments of life. Mostly it's the little unnoticed things—helping clean up the youth room after a big bash; setting out the chairs for a church event; visiting the nursing home and talking quietly with one of the patients; giving your time and money to help the poor in the local city.

God gives us all opportunities to serve. But if we're not ready, we might miss them.

MIND: Look at the following Scriptures and identify

the way that someone served another: Jesus with the leper (Matthew 8:1-4); the deacons (Acts 6:1-6); the jailer (Acts 16:27-34).

MIGHT: How's your serve? Not your tennis serve, but your personal willingness to give? Think of someone in your family whom you might serve tonight—Mom with the dishes, Dad with the lawn, your little sister with cleaning her room. Are you willing to help out?

TUESDAY: The lowest of the low

HEART: How do you tell others to look at you? Athlete? Big Man on Campus? Homecoming Queen? Scholar? Editor of the Yearbook? Reporter for the News?

Now transpose that to how the Apostle Paul wanted people to see him. You'll find his answer in First Corinthians 4:1: "So then, man ought to regard us as servants of Christ."

"Servants of Christ." It's a nice expression. Pious. Most of us wouldn't mind being called a "servant of Christ." Maybe not just a servant. But the "of Christ" makes it worth it, right?

But do you know what the word was that Paul used here? It's the Greek word for an "underrower." What was that? The Roman galleys (warships) had three levels of oars, each one manned by a rower which sped the ship towards its enemies. If you were a decent fellow, strong and obedient, you might fill a seat on an upper level. But the lowest slaves were dropped through a grate in the upper deck down to the lowest floor. There, they were whipped mercilessly until every bit of strength was poured into their rowing. They were underrowers, the lowest of the low.

SOUL: How does that figure in your outlook? Paul—an underrower, the lowest of the low? Is that how you see yourself? I don't mean in a groveling, demeaning sense. You don't have to go around telling everyone what a miserable cur you are, or that you're nothing, a nobody—useless, stupid, rejected. But Paul saw himself as a mere galley slave for Christ.

How do you see yourself now? It's a tough way to look at life. But that was how Paul viewed himself and it's certainly a principle applicable to all of us.

MIND: Meditate on Paul's words in First Corinthians 4:1-21. What principles can you glean from the apostle's words about serving others?

MIGHT: No job was considered beneath the dignity of a galley slave. Clean up slop? Shovel out the outhouse? Scour the mildew off the wall? They had to do it. No questions asked.

Take a look at your attitude today. Are there jobs you rankle at, things others ask you to do that you consider beneath you? Stop. Take a look at Paul's words. Which would you rather be—a king headed for hell or a galley slave whose name is written in heaven?

WEDNESDAY: "Just a little rock"

HEART: I was driving back to our office from our plant and I suddenly noticed a broken cinder block on the street. I swerved around it and said to myself, "That could tear the bottom out of this car. Glad I saw that."

Then a little voice inside me said, "Right. And it could tear the bottom out of someone else's car, too. Why don't you go heave it out of the road?"

I sighed. "Come on, I have to get back to the office. Let someone else do it."

"Who?"

"I don't know. Just someone."

"Why not you?"

"Well, I . . . uh . . . I don't know. I just don't feel like it."

Whoever it was talking to me—conscience? The Holy Spirit?—kept talking. I finally gave in. I turned around, drove back to the spot, parked, ran out in the road and threw the cinder block out of the way.

Then I stood there waiting for someone to stop and congratulate me!

SOUL: Not really. But something about it felt good.

That's precisely what Scripture tells us will happen when we serve. Paul said, "Now I rejoice in what was suffered for you"(Colossians 1:24). Jesus told His disciples when He washed their feet, "Now that you know these things, you will be blessed if you do them"(John 13:17). The word "blessed" means "happy." Your own true joy will be realized through serving others, not through being served.

MIND: Read and meditate on Galatians 5:13. What does it mean we are "called to be free" but we're not to "use [our] freedom to indulge the sinful nature; rather, serve one another in love"?

MIGHT: Make a deliberate effort today to do some-thing for someone else that you might find dis-tasteful. After all is said and done, analyze your thoughts and feelings. Was there a true sense of joy? Did you sense the blessing of God? Why or why not?

THURSDAY: "I gave you an example"

HEART: The disciples filed into the sparsely fur-nished room. Just a low table, some small rugs. The food had not yet been brought in. Several noted that there was no servant at the door to wash their feet. Peter remarked, "Well, Thomas, I guess I'll have to put up with your smelly feet tonight." Everyone laughed.

But after they'd all taken positions lying around the table, the nauseating smell of unclean feet rose into the air. No one said anything. Several kept shift-ing positions. Jesus looked about at them, saying nothing. The food was brought in. Four steaming bowls of delicious meat. There were loaves of bread, wine and meat. After a prayer, they all dipped eager-ly into the gravy with their bread. But what was that rancid smell? Oh, our feet! Ugh!

Shortly after that first round, Jesus rose and disappeared. Moments later, He stepped back into the
room. He was naked above the waist, a towel
wrapped about His loins and a large pitcher of water
in His hand. He poured it into the basin by the door.
Then He motioned to Thomas to stand and be
washed.

SOUL: How do you think you might have felt to be
Thomas at that moment?

We've heard and read it so often, it's lost its
power. Just the same, imagine having the President
of the United States come to your house so he can
shine your shoes! Or having Jim Kelly, the Buffalo
Bills' quarterback, come by, and instead of showing
you how to throw a spiral, he sews up the hole in
your uniform!

Still, it doesn't come close. Jesus was God,
Creator, Master, Lord. And here He is, cleaning the
dust off the feet of 12 arrogant men.

Could you and I do that?

MIND: Just to fix in your mind how far Jesus was willing to go to serve, read John 13 again. What does
this passage teach about Jesus' service and obedience to the truth?

MIGHT: Try an experiment. The next time someone
asks you to do something special—like do the dishes, cut the lawn, take out the trash—notice your
inner feelings. How gladly did you comply? Was it
easy? Yet, how did you feel afterwards? Was there a

little shine in your heart as you completed the task? That's part of the reward. What's the other part? Maybe you'll hear about that at the judgment seat of Christ!

FRIDAY: The visit

HEART: Edwin Markham wrote a poem called, "The Shoes of Happiness." In it he speaks of how Conrad, an old cobbler, dreamt that one day Jesus would come as a guest to his home. The next morning he rose early and decorated his shoe shop with colorful flowers. He wanted to welcome the Master in style. "When the Master comes," he told himself, I'll wash His feet where the spikes have been and I will kiss the hands that have been punctured by the nails."

But Jesus didn't come.

Instead, an ancient beggar arrived shoeless. Conrad gave him a pair of handmade shoes fitted precisely to his feet. All the while, he looked for Jesus.

Still, Jesus didn't come.

Instead, an old woman walked by with a huge parcel on her back. Conrad lifted the burden off her bent back and gave her a meal. All the while, he kept an eye out for Jesus.

But Jesus didn't come.

Then, just as the sun set, a weeping child came by. Conrad led her back to her mother.

The Jesus Conrad imagined never came that day. But Markham's poem concludes,

Then soft in the silence a voice he heard;

"Lift up your head, for I kept my word.
Three times I came to your friendly door;
Three times my shadow was on your floor.
I was the beggar with bruised feet.
I was the woman you gave to eat.
I was the child in the homeless street."

SOUL: Many variations have been played on that plot. But it's not just a story. It's true. It happens all the time, every day, at your door and mine, in your classes and mine, in the places we meet and talk and eat. Jesus is there. Look into the faces of those around you and you'll see the glimmer of His smile, the long gaze of His love, the willing response of His ear. He's there—if you'll only look.

MIND: Read Hebrews 13:2 and Matthew 25:31-40 for some more insight into this theme.

MIGHT: Do you ever find yourself thinking what you'd do if Jesus came by your house today? We all do at times. Ever think that if you had been there at the cross you wouldn't have run like the other disciples? Have you ever shaken your head about the innkeeper who had no room for Joseph and Mary, thinking you'd have never done such a thing?

Then think again about all those folks you had a chance to serve today. How did you do? Review. How might you have done better?

SATURDAY/SUNDAY: The biscuit the fly sat on

HEART: Many accolades have gone in recent years to Eric Liddell, the Olympic sprinter whose life the movie, *Chariots of Fire*, chronicled. In fact, the movie was in many ways far removed from the truth. Liddell never ran against Harold Abrahams (the other star in the movie). Nor did he have an acute battle over running on the sabbath. That issue was decided long before he ever got to the Olympics. He said he wouldn't run on a Sunday without, apparently, a hint of doubt or a microsecond of struggle. I'd recommend Sally Magnuson's book, *The Flying Scotsman,* if you're interested in a fuller treatment of Liddell's life. In it you'll find some interesting stories about Eric. But there's one that always interested me.

At a coffee, someone noticed a fly leaving its dirty tracks all over one of the biscuits. He mentioned it to Eric, knowing he'd want to avoid the germs. But in fact, "this was the biscuit Eric was careful to take," said the storyteller. "His action was not intended as a rebuke to me—that would never occur to him—but to make certain that no one else should suffer discomfort as a result of eating a biscuit defiled by a fly" (*The Flying Scotsman*, by Sally Magnuson, Quartet Books, New York, 1981, page 103).

SOUL: I think that's the mark of true servanthood— serving even when others probably won't notice (even though in this case someone did). Serving when you know there will be no "honorable mention," no "plaque awarded to numero uno," no "monetary reward on the side" is true service, the kind God Himself praises.

MIND: Read John 2:1-11 and weigh in particular the fact that this was Jesus' first miracle, the first thing He would do as the Messiah.

MIGHT: If you were going to choreograph Jesus' first day as the Messiah, how would you start it off? What miracles would you begin with? Why do you think Jesus began with this one? Use Jesus as an example of the best in servanthood. Try to think of something you can do which no one but God will know about. Then do it.

6

I Could Sure Use a Compliment Today

Therefore encourage one another and build each other up, just as in fact you are doing.
1 Thessalonians 5:11

MONDAY: "We thank you for your support."

HEART: Perhaps you've seen the commercial on television where the two old-timers sell a new wine cooler. Product aside, I have to admit I like the way the speaker always ends his little talk: "And we thank you for your support."

Clever ending, yes. But it's really just ad hype. Real support is hard to come by—but it's not impossible.

When General Douglas MacArthur left Corregidor in 1942, to flee from the Japanese, he assured his men, "I shall return." Lt. General Jonathan Wainwright was left on the island as commanding officer. After a hard and long fight, Wainwright had to surrender. He spent the next three years as a prisoner of war in Manchuria.

71

In 1945 MacArthur's reinforcements liberated him and his men. But by then Wainwright was a broken man. He was haggard and could not walk without a cane. The day came when he faced his old commanding officer. MacArthur was eager to talk to him, but Wainwright was embarrassed and humiliated, considering himself a disgrace. He was convinced he'd never get another command. When Gen. MacArthur talked with Wainwright, he was shocked and horrified. Nothing but thoughts of compassion and love filled his mind. His first words to the defeated General were, "Why, Jim, your old corps is yours when you want it."

The moment MacArthur finished, Wainwright's voice broke. He said, "General . . . ," and burst into tears.

SOUL: Throughout world history, people and nations have stood or fallen on the basis of words spoken in difficult circumstances. King Solomon had an expression for it: "A word aptly spoken is like apples of gold in settings of silver."(Proverbs 25:11).

Undoubtedly, the king had delighted in the delicious golden-hued apples brought to him in silver baskets. Their aroma stimulated the nostrils; their meat filled the stomach. Our words have the same power— to build up or break down, to kindle a fire in the heart or kill a gleam in the soul.

MIND: Read these passages for examples of where Christians supported others: Second Timothy 1:3-14; Acts 16:23-34; and Luke 10:38-42.

MIGHT: Take a look around at the people in your lunch room. Whom do you think might need a little lift, a word of support? Write a name down now. What could you say to them that might provide that "apple of gold" today?

TUESDAY: This is your moment!

HEART: I read the words with a pounding heart. It was almost as if I had been transported back through time nearly 36 years. June 4, 1940. London. The House of Commons. Winston Churchill delivering a speech designed to turn a haggard, hopeless nation around.

I could imagine the gravelly English voice growling out the astounding words.

"We shall not flag or fail. We shall fight in France, we shall fight on the seas and oceans, we shall fight with growing confidence and growing strength in the air . . . "

The words ignited a fuse in my soul. I could almost imagine myself a dour English farmer or businessman listening to the "wireless," the whole family crowded about on chairs and leaning forward to catch every clause. Memories of Hitler's bombs and the juggernaut that had routed the Allies' best armies through France and Belgium were still fresh in their minds.

"We shall defend our island, whatever the cost may be, we shall fight on the beaches, we shall fight on the landing grounds. . . "

I could almost hear the pounding of the guns, the thumpthump of bombs in the distance as I listened. I felt lifted, billowed up on some strange, almost supernatural hand. Where had Churchill found such words?

"We shall fight in the fields and in the streets, we shall fight in the hills. . . "

I could hear the pause. I could see the great bulldog face and fiery eyes gazing out over the Commons. Somehow nearly every eye meets his. Then the fist comes out, and down.

BANG!

"We shall never surrender!"

The words still had power, even then in 1976. I was 26 years old. I hadn't even been born when Churchill spoke, but the words were still fresh today. I felt encouraged to face my own battles with help from God and others.

SOUL: We tend to think of such moments as "once in a lifetime" opportunities. Perhaps. But the Apostle Paul didn't see it that way. He saw every day, every hour of the day as an opportunity for a lasting victory. He put it this way: "For we are God's workmanship, created in Christ Jesus to do good works, which God prepared in advance for us to do"(Ephesians 2:10). "Good works." Call them opportunities, "moments." Not just being a Boy Scout, or helping a little old lady across the street. But ripe, golden chances to do good, to do right. To help. To give. To light a life. To lighten a load. To encourage. Paul saw that God prepared every life with thousands, perhaps millions, of such opportunities.

MIND: Here are several Scriptures that remind us we are here to live lives full of good works: Titus 2:14; Titus 3:14; 3 John 5-8; Ephesians 2:10.

MIGHT: A moment comes every day—once, maybe twice, perhaps three times—to do good, to help, to lend a hand, to give, to open yourself up to a friend, a teacher or a hurting student. God is always abundant in His mercies. Will you strike fire or strike out?

WEDNESDAY: "Then don't!"

HEART: I was profoundly depressed, fearful that I'd never amount to anything. I was studying for the ministry at a well-known seminary, but something inside me kept saying I was a nothing, a failure, I'd never succeed.

One day in the car, I poured out my fears to my mother. She appeared frustrated, then angry, then caring all at once. Suddenly she said to me, "Do you know how Franklin Roosevelt got into politics?" I said no. She replied, "He had suffered from polio as a child, and was convinced the fact that he was crippled prevented him from trying anything. Then he met his future wife, Eleanor. They were married, and she encouraged him. She told him to run for governor of New York. He went back and forth about it for months. Finally, one day she asked him what he was waiting for. He said he was afraid. 'Afraid of what?' she asked. 'Afraid I'll fail,' he answered. Eleanor was silent. Finally she said, 'Then don't.'"

My mother looked me in the eye. She said, "So

you tell me you're afraid of failure? You know what I say—Don't. Don't fail. Give it your best effort. Quit worrying about failing and get in there and try."

It was a classic pep talk. But it struck home. Sometimes people need that one encouraging push to keep them keeping on.

SOUL: A memorable moment of my life. One where someone's words kept me going. As we've discussed so far, there are different ways to encourage people. One is through supportive words and reassuring words. There are also empowering words. As Proverbs says, "The tongue has the power of life and death, and those who love it will eat its fruit"(18:21).

MIND: There are some empowering words in Scripture that you should know. Try Second Peter 1:2-4, Ephesians 3:20-21 and Matthew 28:18-20.

MIGHT: What power do you find in these words from Scripture? Are you afraid of failing, looking the fool, being put down? What power do these words give you for the rigors you face? Write down one thought from these Scriptures that you need to remind yourself of today. Put it on a card and keep it in a handy pocket. Periodically pull those words out and speak them to yourself.

THURSDAY: "Speak the truth!"

HEART: The Olympics. 1924. The 400 meters. A grueling race. A dash like the hundred meters, but long distance like the mile. All out for 400 meters, 400 paces. Your chest heaves. Your whole body begins to erupt.

Eric Liddell faced that moment. The gun would soon roar and he would fire forth, pressing every ounce of muscle and strength towards that tape. But he had an ally on his side, something no one else had in that race. It was a precious truth. The athletics masseur who attended to the British team had found a special heart in Eric. It had come out of his valiant desire to honor God and not break the sabbath by running on a Sunday. He'd forfeited his best event—the hundred meters—and decided to run the 400, something he had not made a major mark in. The masseur wrote him a note before he went to the line that day. It said, "In the old book it says, 'He that honours Me I will honour.' Wishing you the best of success always."

God had spoken. The gun resounded. Liddell bounded forth.

SOUL: If you've seen the movie, *Chariots of Fire*, you know the outcome of that race. Liddell won. What you may not know is that it was considered the race of the 1924 Paris Games. Liddell's ungainly, convulsive running style won the hearts of many who observed. His running was wild, all out, abandoned—to the glory of his Lord and truth.

I wonder if those words that masseur gave him at the last moment were just the spiritual push he needed to run his race. Surely he had honored God. Now it was the Lord's chance to honor him. And He did.

MIND: Truth. Do you know it's power? What is the power of God's word? Read such Scriptures as Hebrews 4:12, Second Timothy 3:16-17, Romans 15:4 and Psalm 119:1-16, 97-100.

MIGHT: Nothing can encourage a person like God's truth. What words of God do you treasure? What words resound in your soul when you're afraid, or down or feeling hopeless? Stop now and pray. Ask the Lord for an opportunity to share with someone a word from God that has struck you. What is that word? Write it down and prepare for the opportunity God gives you today.

FRIDAY: "I believe in you!"

HEART: Peter stands there, casting a net. He calls to Andrew, "Over there. Pull it in over there." As he casts the net, he wonders about this new prophet who has appeared, Jesus. Who was He? Peter wonders. Could He be the Messiah?

He continues casting the net and pulling it in. Out of the corner of his eye, though, he notices a man walking towards him. He glances behind him, then flinches. It's Jesus, he says to himself. He begins to shake. What does He want with me? Peter thinks. He quivers and waits, continuing to pull on the net.

Jesus calls him. "Simon. Simon!"

Peter shifts his weight, then looks up at Him. "Yes, Master?"

Jesus glances at the net. "Not much of a catch today?"

Peter nods.

Jesus gazes at Andrew, then back at Peter. His eyes are quiet, peaceful, yet drawing. Peter's heart resounds inside him. Momentarily he wishes he had the time to be with Jesus, to listen to Him. But . . .

Suddenly Jesus says, "Peter, Andrew, follow Me. I will make you fishers of men."

Peter gulps. He feels Andrew's eyes on him. Then without hesitation, he drops his net, walks out of the water. Jesus has already moved up the beach. He follows.

SOUL: What a marvelous promise: "Follow me and I will make you fishers of men." You'll find it in Mark 1:17. It was Jesus' invitation to Peter and Andrew, mere fishermen. But Jesus' words said something far greater and deeper. This: "I believe in you; I trust you; I can make you into something you can only dream about. All you have to do is follow Me." Do you have anyone who believes in you like that?

MIND: If you don't know of such a person, you're not thinking because Jesus says the same thing to you. Look at these verses and think what encouragement they offer to you personally: Jude 24-25; John 7:37-39; Matthew 11:28-30.

MIGHT: Did you ever think that just as you are called to "believe" in Jesus, He also "believes" in you? That is, He has complete confidence you will become what He plans to make of you. Look at the verses listed for today. Which one strikes you strongest? Memorize it. Whom might you share this verse with today in your own family? Tell them what it means to you, how it has affected you.

SATURDAY/SUNDAY: Acceptance

HEART: During the last Allied offensive of World War II, General Dwight Eisenhower bumped into a G.I. pacing by the Rhine River during a foggy twilight evening. There was never any superiority about the general. He simply asked, "What's the matter, soldier?"

The young man didn't recognize the Supreme Allied Commander. Perhaps he was too afraid and caught up in his own thoughts. But he replied, "I guess I'm a little nervous."

The general paused, then answered with characteristic humility, "Well, so am I. Let's both walk together by the river and perhaps we'll draw strength from each other."

SOUL: One thing most of us crave more than anything in this world is acceptance, a sense that we're not alone in our feelings, our struggles. Each of us has the power to make a person feel accepted and loved by what we say and how we treat them. Gen. Eisenhower accomplished that with that young soldier.

At the same time, we need to know how God accepts us. Perhaps Paul's words in Romans 8:1 will help: "Therefore there is now no condemnation for those who are in Christ Jesus." No condemnation! Nothing against us. Total acceptance.

MIND: Do you feel accepted by God? If not, read these Scriptures to find out what He says about you: Psalms 139:13-16; Jeremiah 33:3; Jeremiah 29:11-13; Second Timothy 1:7.

MIGHT: Do you know of someone who appears to feel unloved, unaccepted, uncared about? Someone who may feel alone, weighed down under the burdens they're living with? Who is that person? Write down their name. Perhaps you might write them a note, expressing your love, and telling them how one of these Scriptures or another has helped you. Why not do it today?

7

I Positively Refuse to Do What He Says

Submit to one another out of reverence for Christ.
Ephesians 5:21

MONDAY: The dirty word

HEART: If there's any single dirty non-four letter word in the English language, it's got to be the word, "submission." What images does the word "submit" bring up in your mind?

The beaten dog, tail between its legs, cowering before its master?

The schoolboy, just chewed out by his teacher, hanging his head while others laugh at him?

The employee, punctuating every one of his boss' remarks with a "Yes, sir"?

The private, stiffly saluting his sergeant and sighing as he heads off for latrine duty?

The tired mother with vacant eyes and sunken cheeks listening to her husband's tirade about the burned steak for the sixth time this week?

We tend to put a negative sign in front of the word, don't we? But is that the way it's supposed to be? Is that what God meant when He told us through Paul, "Submit to one another out of reverence for Christ"(Ephesians 5:21)?

SOUL: The essence of submission is obedience. The word literally means, "put yourself under" another's authority or need. Do what they request. Oblige them. And do it with joy.

That's not easy. Warren Wiersbe has written that there are three levels of obedience. Number one, the "fear" stage is when we obey because we don't want to have to be punished for not obeying. Number two is the "reward" stage—we obey because we get something out of it—money, a gift, a token, free time—something. But the third stage is the one the Lord seeks in all of us, the "love" stage—obeying because we love Christ and our fellow Christians.

Putting yourself under another's authority and meeting their need is the essence of submission to the Lordship of Christ. When we submit to others out of love for Jesus, it's as though we're doing it for Jesus.

MIND: Read the context of Ephesians 5:15-6:9, noting the position of verse 21, "submit to one another out of reverence for Christ." Why do you think Paul's message about being "filled with the Spirit" is followed immediately by a number of relationships in the home and at work?

MIGHT: How do you picture yourself—

    happy-go-lucky?
    generally obedient?
    rebellious to authority?
    a "grin and bear it" type of person?
    one who "goes with the flow"?

Discuss with someone close to you how you come across when you have to submit to someone else— a teacher, a parent, a friend. How do they see you?

TUESDAY: "Honor them?! Come on!"

HEART: One of the first areas in which the Bible speaks of submission is children to parents. It's the fifth of the ten commandments: "Honor your father and mother." Paul amplifies it in Ephesians 6:1-3: "Children, obey your parents in the Lord, for this is right. 'Honor your father and mother'—which is the first commandment with a promise—'that it may go well with you, and that you may enjoy long life on the earth.' "

SOUL: Ever get in on a conversation like this?
  "Mickey?"
  "Yes, Mom?"
  "You were going to cut the lawn today."
  "Aw, Mom, the grass isn't that long, and anyway, Bill and I were going to go over to Sam's house and . . ."
  "You know what happens when you put it off,

Mick. Now get hopping and it'll be done before you know it."

"Mom, I promise I'll do it tomorrow afternoon. Right after school."

"I want it done today."

"Come on, Mom, give me a break."

"Mickey, do I have to get your father involved in this?"

Mick sighs and grits his teeth, muttering under his breath. He goes out to cut the lawn, but he feels angry, and as he pushes the lawnmower he develops a headache. By the time he's done, he feels the afternoon is ruined.

MIND: Could Mickey have gone about that job with a different attitude? Would a different attitude have changed the whole nature of the work? Read Luke 22:39-53 for some insight into the attitude of Christ about a job no one would relish.

MIGHT: There's an old story about Michelangelo, the great Italian painter, when he was commissioned by the Pope to paint the Sistine Chapel. Michelangelo was old, tired, and in no shape for the arduous work. When the Pope called him, he protested. But his patrons in Florence told him to obey his leader. When he arrived at the Vatican, the Pope laid out his marvelous plan for the Sistine ceiling. Nonetheless, the great painter begged to be let off. He was old, arthritic; he couldn't lie on his back for hours on the high scaffolds laying out the intricate work, let alone painting in the layered fresco style. His eyes were bad.

Nonetheless, the Pope said, "You are the greatest architect, sculptor and painter, and one of the great poets of the age. Your church calls upon you for this last supreme effort."

Michelangelo knew he was beaten. His final answer was in the customary language of the day: "Okay, boss, whassa color you want?"

Are you smiling? I hope so. Sometimes the best way to face a tough task is to inject a little humor into it and then proceed.

WEDNESDAY: God has ways of making you.

HEART: Ever see a sheep? They can be ornery, can't they? I've often wondered how a shepherd could watch over a whole flock of a hundred or so and keep them moving. But they have their ways.

A traveler in the Swiss Alps came upon such a shepherd weeping with a lamb in his lap. The lamb's leg was broken and the shepherd was trying to comfort it. The traveler's heart was moved and he asked how it had happened. The shepherd said that he had broken the lamb's leg himself.

The traveler was aghast, but the shepherd explained, "This lamb is one of the most wayward in the whole flock. Every time I take the sheep out to graze, he leads others away from the flock too close to the cliffs. He would wander with smaller lambs and get lost. I have to teach him to obey and I'm doing it by breaking his leg. Until it heals, I'll carry him myself. And when he can walk again, he will be one of the most loyal and obedient lambs of all."

SOUL: That story is every Christian's story. God disciplines us to teach us to obey. Even Jesus "learned obedience from what He suffered" (Hebrews 5:8). God teaches us to submit to others by putting us in situations where we learn to do it. We can learn it the easy way or the hard way, but He's capable of developing us either way.

MIND: Which way are you learning to submit to others? Study the words of Ruth in Ruth 1:1-18, with particular emphasis on her speech to Naomi in verses 16-17. Why do you think Ruth was so willing to submit to her mother-in-law, even when her mother-in-law didn't require or ask it of her?

MIGHT: What is God teaching you about submission in your home, in your church, in your school? Do you see any important principles coming out of the circumstances of life? What do you think might help in giving you a sense of joy in submitting to others?

THURSDAY: Obey your leaders

HEART: Another important area of submission for Christians is to their leaders. Sometimes Christians get the idea that the main thing in the Christian life is worship, fellowship and spending time with the Lord personally. These are all important. But there are other elements, too.

If you've ever played on a team—football, basketball, field hockey, volleyball—you'll identify with the
following illustration. Suppose your coach gathered all
the members of the team into the locker room and
had a strategy session.

The coach says to the starting quarterback,
"Smith, we're going with the T formation today. I'll
have you call plays in the second quarter if we do
well in the first. But in the first quarter, I'll call all the
plays."

The coach turns to his three backfield men. "Bailey
and Barney will rotate on the plays. After each down,
the one on the field will come out and the other
will come in with the new play. Got it?"

Everyone nods.

He looks at his four pass receivers. "Simpson,
Morgan. Listen up. I want you to cut those outs
tight today. And when you're in on the line, Simpson,
I want to see some tough blocking. You understand?"

Apparently, Simpson's been flaking off a little.
So he raises his hand. But imagine he says the following: "Coach, this has been a great session today.
But I was thinking, why do we have to go out and play
on that field. I mean, it's dirty, our new uniforms will
get stained. And we'll all be hurting on Sunday. Why
don't we just stay in here and have some real good
fellowship. That's what it's all about, isn't it—us
relating to you and learning from you?"

What might that coach say? "Are you nuts,
Simpson? There will be plenty of time for fellowship
after the game. But right now there's a job to do. Now
let's get to it!"

SOUL: That may look at little ridiculous to you, but that's how too many of us come at obedience and submission. We forget that God wants us engaged in battle, not always on the sidelines in "quiet" strategy sessions. He desires that we obey our leaders—in the home, church and school. That's just as important as other things like fellowship, worship and witnessing. He wants us to get the mission acomplished. Don't mix up those elements of the Christian life. Worship and fellowship are important. But so is submission. Keep them in balance.

MIND: Read Jesus' words in Luke 6:46 and Matthew 7:21-23. How high a premium do you think the Lord puts on obedience? Now read First Samuel 15:22-23, Hebrews 13:17 and First Peter 5:5 for more insight.

MIGHT: Step back and take a look at yourself in relation to your leaders. How often do you grumble about things they ask you to do? How often do you argue, or even refuse to obey? From the Scriptures you read above, how do you think the Lord regards such behavior?

FRIDAY: The only time not to obey

HEART: Our age has seen an outpouring of evil unlike any time in history. World War I killed millions. World War II added to the numbers, then piled an additional 6 million Jews and 6 million others exterminated by Hitler and his hateful hordes. What astonishes historians is how obedient the Germans were to Hitler, even though many of them now admit what he asked of them was demonic.

How would you respond if asked to obey a command that would lead to great pain and anguish for someone else?

SOUL: Perhaps you can't answer. But an experiment conducted at Yale University by Dr. Stanley Milgram shows us just how far some people will obey even murderous commands. The studies involved three people—a "learner," a "teacher" and an "experimenter," or authority figure. The teacher subjected the learner to a series of questions. If the learner answered incorrectly, the teacher had to shock him with a charge of electricity, up to 450 volts. The intensity of the charge was determined by the experimenter. There was one thing, though, that the "teacher" didn't know: he was really the one being tested.

You see, the "learners" in each case were actors who pretended to be responding to real electrical charges. But there was no real jolt. They often answered questions wrong just to force the teacher to have to give higher charges or punishments. The shock levels were labeled from "Slight shock" all the way up to "Danger: severe shock" and "XXX."

When the learner answered a question incorrectly, the teacher was to flip the shock switch. The learner would respond to the shocks with screams, pleading, statements like "I have a heart problem" and so on. But the teacher was told to ignore this. If when the victim acted like this the teacher refused to administer more shocks, the experimenter said, "Please go on." If he balked again, the experimenter said, "The experiment requires that you continue." This went on through five refusals. If after five, the teacher continued to refuse to shock the learner as required, the experiment was over.

You might think that most people chose not to administer severe shocks.

Not so. Sixty-five percent of the time the teacher went all the way into XXX shocks!

MIND: How does this relate to Christian obedience? There are times when we are not to obey or submit to those over us. When does that happen? Read about Peter and John in Acts 4:13-22, paying particular attention to verses 19-20.

MIGHT: When do you believe that an authority in this world is to be disobeyed? Have you ever been in such a situation? What did you do? Why did you do it? Could this even happen in the church or the home? What kinds of situations can you imagine happening that might call for such action?

SATURDAY/SUNDAY:
Keep on keeping on

HEART: If you're like me, you often feel as though your efforts at obedience, love, reaching out and giving are overlooked, downplayed, ridiculed or even forgotten entirely. But we don't have our eyes set on the things of earth, but the truths of heaven—right?

There's a story about a man who had a dream. He was told by God to split a giant granite rock. He was banging away at it with his pick, but nothing happened. Finally, after much effort, he stopped. "It's useless. I'll never break the rock."

Suddenly, an angel stood by him in his dream. The angel said, "Weren't you given a job to do? If so, why have you stopped?"

The worker replied, "The work is useless. I can't make any impression on the rock."

The angel replied, "What's that to you? Your duty is to bang away at the rock, whether it breaks or not. The work is yours. The results are in other hands. Therefore, work on."

In the dream, he sighed and hoisted the pick over his head. With one blow, the whole rock split cleanly.

SOUL: Are you asking yourself, "What use is it? I never see any results?"

You're in good company. Probably every Christian who has ever lived has asked those questions.

MIND: Maybe Galatians 6:9-10 will help. Read those verses and think how they apply to your situation. Then turn to First Corinthians 15:58.

MIGHT: "Your labor in the Lord is not in vain." "Vain" means emptiness. Worthlessness. Uselessness. But that's not what God designed us for. Oh, in this world it may look like our efforts at doing good and submitting to others are accomplishing little. But

don't look with worldly eyes. Look with the spiritual
eyes of discernment. It's by filling our minds with the
truth like the verses mentioned above that we get
such eyes. Why not memorize both passages—this
week?

8

You're Messin' Up, Bill

I myself also am convinced that you yourselves are full of goodness, filled with all knowledge, and able also to admonish one another.

Romans 15:14, NASB

MONDAY: "I'd like to give him a good piece of my mind!"

HEART: Have you ever heard yourself uttering words like that?

"Oh, I wouldn't have any trouble telling him off!"

"I'm going to let him have it. Today's the day."

"If she says one more thing, I'm going to explode."

"He's such a hypocrite. How can he call himself a Christian and do that?"

There's a proper biblical process for dealing with friends, church members and other Christians who sin. It's called church discipline. The writer to the Hebrews said, "Endure hardship as discipline" (Hebrews 12:7). Part of the reason any of us are even here is because God is transforming us. Much of that transformation comes through others telling us the truth—"admonishing," as Paul says in Romans 15:14.

SOUL: What is it to "admonish?"

The Greek word here is *noutheteo*. It's a picturesque word, as many Greek (and English) words are. It means to give instruction or warn with the idea of turning someone back from foolish or sinful behavior.

Ever meet someone who likes to "tell people off"?

That's not biblical admonishment. One who truly admonishes seeks to accomplish something good for the person he's speaking to. His goal is not simply to "let them have it," or to "set them straight once and for all." Rather, it's to help, to restore, to rebuild a life. Anyone can do it—even young children.

I dressed my daughter this morning. We were in a hurry, so I was a little rough. She said to me, "Daddy, that hurts."

I replied, "No it doesn't. If you'd just . . . "

"Daddy, please be gentle."

"Honey, I'm just trying to get you ready. Now please . . . "

"OUCH!"

Later on, she said to me, "Daddy, please try to be nicer to me." It wasn't the most eloquent warning I ever received. But it made the point

That's admonishment—simple, direct, without embellishment. She was kind about it, too, and gentle herself.

MIND: Read Galatians 6:1 for some insight into the process of confrontation and admonishment. What steps do you see in the process?

MIGHT: How do you approach someone you feel is sinning or has sinned? Do you feel the anger welling up inside you till you're about to explode? Do you hyperventilate, afraid they might strike you or spit in your face? Or are you so confident you feel as though you can stride right up to them and "let them have it with both barrels"? If so, you're doing a number of things wrong. In the following lessons we'll look at this important issue and try to reach some conclusions.

TUESDAY: Full of goodness

HEART: Are you competent to admonish?

Bill was nervous about what he was about to say to his father. He had such a temper. Three times he'd walked into the living room where Dad was reading the paper, and three times he'd turned around to walk out. He couldn't work up the nerve.

Finally he called Tom, his friend and an older Christian. "What do I do? How do I say it?"

Tom asked, "Have you looked at yourself first, Bill?"

"What do you mean?"

"Are you walking with the Lord yourself? Are you living a clean life before Him? Remember, you're going to talk to your dad about his mouth around the house—how he swears so much and loses his temper. What about you? Will he be able to come back at you with a line like, 'Let him who is without sin cast the first stone'?"

"But then I'd have to be perfect."

"No, just fessed up. Have you gotten the deck clear in your own life? Are there any sins you haven't yet dealt with?"

Bill stopped and thought. "Well, there is one thing." He told him about failing to fill up the car with gas after he'd used half a tank the previous weekend.

"Perhaps you ought to approach your dad with an offer to pay then, and after you've gotten that cleared away, you can talk about this other thing."

SOUL: The first thing anyone needs to consider in admonishing another Christian is himself. Paul told the Romans they were competent to admonish because they were "full of goodness." In other words, they were leading godly, holy lives. They were in step with the Lord. They weren't practicing sin, nor did they have past sins still hanging out on the public washline.

MIND: Read Galatians 5:19-21 for a list of sins that all of us commit from time to time. Perhaps Paul's words will remind you of something you need to take care of.

MIGHT: Tom's advice to Bill above was good and wise. In Galatians 6:1 Paul advises "you who are spiritual" to confront erring members of the body. In fact, that "you" is plural. Though the first step of any confrontation is personal and private, in some cases it's wise to consider whether more than one is necessary. But regardless of numbers, that "spirituality" element is crucial. We can't point out a speck in someone's eye when we've got a boulder in our eye.

WEDNESDAY: "Complete in knowledge"

HEART: "Okay," said Tom. "Now, are you sure you're father's sinning?"

Bill reeled back. "Isn't it clear? Swearing. Outbursts of anger. Man, we can barely stand it in this house. My mom is so afraid of him—and he calls himself a Christian."

"Well, Bill, remember you need to make sure you understand why you think he's sinning and where it says he is in Scripture. Then it's the word speaking to him, not just you and your opinion."

Bill shook his head. "That's interesting. You mean in a sense that takes the heat off me, because then he has to deal with what the Bible says."

"Right."

"Do you have any Scriptures I can start with?"

SOUL: Tom was leading Bill in the right direction. You can't confront someone about sin unless you're clear it's sin. There are many "gray areas" in life, matters over which we have the right to pick and choose. Dancing, card-playing, wearing makeup, the length of women's dresses—all those things have been regarded as evil by different groups. But are they scripturally evil, or is it just our opinion?

In Bill's case, his dad used foul language and was abusive in his speech to his family. Anyone can find many Scriptures on those subjects if they'll take the time to look them up. If you believe someone's behavior is sinful, but aren't sure what the Bible says, why not take the time to find out? It could spell the difference between a successful restoration of a sinner and an embarrassing break in relations.

MIND: Paul told the Romans that they were competent because they were also "complete in knowledge." They knew the word of God. Read two important passages that detail what power the word has in a believer's life: Hebrews 4:12 and Second Timothy 3:16-17. What do they tell you about what you need to bring off a successful word of admonishment?

MIGHT: Find two solid verses in Scripture that you think might pertain to Bill's situation above. Put yourself in his shoes. Even if he didn't bring out the Bible to show his dad (so as not to look like the "Great White Teacher" or something), at least he'd be sure of his basis for speaking to him.

THURSDAY: Genuine concern

HEART: Bill found several Scriptures relating to his father's conduct. He called Tom back and read them to him. Then he said, "Man, I feel like David going up against Goliath!"

"Whoa!" exclaimed Tom.

"Whaddaya mean, 'Whoa!' I feel confident now."

"That brings us to another issue, Bill. What should be your attitude in approaching your dad? Open up to Galatians 6:1."

Bill found the passage and read. "I'm supposed to approach him with a spirit of gentleness."

"Amen," said Tom. "That means humility, love, kindness, all those things. Is that the way you're coming at this?"

"I guess not."

"Maybe you need to pray about your attitude then."

SOUL: I've been in many confrontations in my short life. Some of them have been wonderful steps to growth and development in Christ. And some of them have been the most down moments of my life. In several that I remember the biggest problem was my attitude. I did feel like David going up against Goliath in several situations. And my goal was to knock my opponent down and out!

But that's all wrong, isn't it?

We're to come at it with an attitude of gentleness. With the goal of restoration. With the purpose of helping and healing, not destroying.

MIND: Read about Nathan's confrontation of David in Second Samuel 12:1-15. How do you see Nathan's approach in relation to Galatians 6:1 and Matthew 18:15-17 (another passage about confrontation)?

MIGHT: Attitude is at least as important as approach in speaking with someone whom you believe has sinned. You go with a heart of love, even if at the time you may be a little angry. Being angry doesn't mean you don't care. In fact, you can be sure there will be some emotion in such a situation. When I was a pastor, I had a man in my congregation who struggled daily with alcoholism. Since he worked at night, he spent his morning hours in the local bar. I had been working with him and his wife in the mornings by teaching them to spend time in the Scriptures. But because of my schedule, we stopped doing it for awhile and he slipped back into his habits.

When I found out about it, I was angry. I drove over to the bar he was in and stalked in. He greeted me joyously and offered to buy me a Coke. I told him he was drunk, he shouldn't be drinking, and I gave him my business card. I wrote a verse reference on the back of it that said drunks would not inherit the kingdom of God (from First Corinthians 6:9-10). Then I stalked out.

He was outraged about that little episode and we didn't talk for about three months. But my heart was convicted. I had touted him as a trophy in my church, but I wasn't treating him with love. I went to his house one day, found him sober and we had a good talk. I apologized for my actions and told him that I cared and I wanted to see him stand on his own, as the head of a wholesome family. He repented, later went into a hospital program for alcoholics and came out restored.

But it was a good lesson. I realized my need to

have a right attitude, even in the midst of anger.

FRIDAY: Leave the results in God's hands

HEART: As Bill worked through his feelings towards his dad, he realized he did care, and that it was love for him that pushed him to take this step. He told Tom, "I think I'm ready."

"Have you prepared what you'll say—as precisely as possible?"

"Yes, I've even written some of it down."

"Do you know what Scriptures to use?"

"Got them memorized."

"What will you do if he argues with you or gets angry?"

Bill swallowed. "I don't know. I keep hoping that won't happen."

"But what if it does?"

"I don't know. I guess I'm afraid we'll just have another big fight."

"That exactly what you don't want to do."

"Well, what do I do then?"

"This: tell him you simply want to say something. It's important that you say it all without his comments. And then when you're done, he can respond. In a way, you're trying to establish some rules for yourself and him. That way, you both agree you're there to talk and listen, not to fight."

"All right. But what if he really loses it?"

"Decide now that you won't. No matter what the provocation. Ask the Lord to help you. If he becomes abusive, tell him you have to leave the room. That's all."

Bill swallowed. "All right."

He said goodbye and walked to the top of the stairs, listening for any sounds downstairs in the living room.

SOUL: Are you a little nervous about this, too? I am. It's not a pleasant experience, confronting someone. But it's critical for all of us to learn to do it. The whole idea is to learn to "speak the truth in love." We want to give them the truth. And we want to do it in a loving way. Is that your goal? Do you believe that's Bill's goal, too?

MIND: Read Ephesians 4:14-16 for more insight into the process of speaking the truth in love, admonition and confrontation. Do you have any more insight into Bill's situation that might help?

MIGHT: Bill will in a few moments walk into the lion's den. What do you think will happen?

Now stop a moment. Notice what I said—"lion's den"? Is that the way you've been thinking of this situation? If you have, perhaps we need to remember one more thing about Bill's dad in there. He's human too—right? He's got feelings. He hurts. He has needs. He struggles. Maybe he's already felt very convicted about this whole problem and Bill's words will come as no surprise. Maybe he feels sick of himself, ready to quit. Or maybe he's an insensitive lion, just wanting to pounce on someone, anyone, who crosses him.

Still, that's an important step. How often do you put yourself in the shoes of the other guy and see how you're coming across to him? Before you take the step of admonishing someone, walk in his moccasins for a few minutes in your mind. It may prepare you for something altogether different.

SATURDAY/SUNDAY: Leave the convicting to God

HEART: Bill walked into the living room. His father was reading the paper in his easy chair. They were alone.

Bill tiptoed up. "Dad?"

His father's voice grunted behind the paper. "Yeah?"

"Can we talk about something?"

There was a long silence. Then, "What?" The paper came down a few inches so that Bill could see his face.

"I wanted to apologize to you about not putting gas in the car last weekend. I . . . ."

"You always do that. You know it's a real pain to come out on Monday morning and have an empty tank just when I'm already late for work."

Bill hung his head a little. "I know. That's why I'm sorry. I won't do it again, and I'll take it out and fill it tonight to make up for it. Is that fair?"

His father stared at Bill, his eyes nearly wide with wonder. Then he shook the paper a moment. "All right. Suit yourself." He turned back to the sports page.

SOUL: How's it going? You think he's doing all right? I'm rooting for him. But I have to admit, his dad is not easy.

"Dad?" Bill said again. "There's something else."

His father pulled the paper down and let out an exasperated sigh. "Okay, what now?"

Bill said, "Please, I know you're tired and all. But let me just say what I want to say. Will you let me do that?"

His father leaned back and eyed him up and down. For a moment, Bill felt a surge of confidence. His father seemed to be listening. He had his attention.

"All right. Lay it on me."

Bill took a deep breath. "It's about some of the language you've been using around the house."

"What the . . ."

Bill held up his hand. "Please, Dad, let me finish. I just don't think you or me or any of us who say we're Christians should talk like that to one another. It angers me. And I know Sharon and Gil don't like it. And Mom's practically pulling her hair out. But . . . "

His father's face was red. Bill knew he was angry. But he was keeping his peace. For now. Bill decided to plunge on.

"But I'm speaking for myself. No one else. I for one would like to see you stop with the cursewords and the bursts of anger and all that. Please. For the family's sake. For Mom's sake. For Gil and Sharon's sake."

His father looked down at the paper. For a moment, Bill thought he shuddered. But he didn't lose his composure.

"Dad," said Bill, "for Jesus' sake. For His sake will you try to stop? I'll help. I'll pray. I'll do anything. Dad . . ."

His father looked up and breathed deeply.

"I love you, Dad."

There was a long difficult silence. Bill didn't know what to say. He felt wrung out.

Then his father said, "I know you do, Bill. I'll work on it."

He let his eyes rest on Bill's face. Then he said, "Thanks."

Bill smiled. He felt like leaping, but he simply stood there. "Guess I'll go fill up that gas tank."

His dad nodded.

MIND: I guess that's what you'd call a happy ending. But there are many confrontations that can go like that. Read about another one that went well in Luke 10:38-42 between the Lord Jesus and Martha. God is in the business of making happy endings.

MIGHT: You and I realize that I as the writer had complete control over my characters. I could make Bill and Bill's dad do anything I wanted—that is, at least, in character. So you might be tempted to think it was too pat, even contrived. I hope not. You see, just as I could lead my characters in my story, so the Lord can lead you, your family, and those around you in the story of history. Trust Him. Rely on

Him. Believe that He can and will bring good out of bad circumstances. That's His ultimate expertise.

9

I Can't Believe He Thinks That

Now may the God who gives perseverance and encouragement grant you to be of the same mind with one another according to Christ Jesus.
Romans 15:5, NASB

MONDAY: Scrubdub's final word

HEART: Another note from that master tor-mentor, Scrubdub, to his protegé, Loopole:

Dear Loopole,
The youth leaders want them to be "of the same mind," eh?
No trouble, really. There are three words I'll give you in response: self, self and self. Get them focused on themselves. Selfishness is the key to nearly everything in our struggle. If we ever win this battle with our Enemy Above, it will be a triumph of the self.
Ambition? Push it.
Self-centeredness? Get rid of the word, but remind

them that they can't love anyone until they first love themselves. They'll spend so much time trying to love themselves, they'll forget to love anyone else.

Self-esteem? Ah, beautiful word. Sometimes known as a healthy self-image. In this century, we've accomplished something we never thought possible—having them concentrate so much on personal health, they care nothing for corporate health, body health, group health, team health. It's all me, me, me. (Mind you, I'm not trying to sing).

There are numerous other little selves to push—selfishness, self-involvement, self-actualization, self-hood. They're all good, so long as it's self they're concentrating on and not Him.

But I think you get my drift.

To thine own self be false.

> Be bad,
> Scrubdub

SOUL: If there is one thing Satan desires most for the church, it's disunity, from the elementary grades up, to the elders council down. It's unity that makes a church body most attractive, and it's disunity that makes outsiders say, "The church is like Noah's Ark—if not for the storm outside, you couldn't stand the stench on the inside."

Do you know what a herd of cows does when attacked by wolves? They put their heads in a circle, their hindquarters outside, and, when the wolves attack, they kick the stuffing out of them.

Do you know what a herd of jackasses do when attacked by wolves? They put their heads outside and their hindquarters inside, and, when the wolves attack, they kick the stuffing out of each other.

Some say those are two objective pictures of the church.

Some youth groups are like that. But it shouldn't be. Nor does it have to be.

MIND: Read Paul's words to the Philippians in chapter 2, verses 1-2. What elements do you see in that passage about unity?

MIGHT: While selfishness destroys unity, selflessness builds it. What ways do you see yourself as being selfish (forget about how others are being selfish—we're talking about *you*)? What steps can you take to cease being self-centered and begin to reach out?

TUESDAY: Four part unity

HEART: Paul lists four elements of unity in Philippians 2:2. Look at them. They are:

"being likeminded"
"having the same love"
"being one in spirit"
"being one in purpose."

What do these expressions mean? Does "being likeminded" imply we shouldn't think for ourselves? Does "being one in purpose" mean I should jettison any personal plans or goals I might set for myself?

Does unity require that we all be alike, that everyone in the church think, speak and act the same every day in every way?

SOUL: Paul was not eliminating any of our freedom to think, feel or act individually. However, what the individualism people in America often espouse is definitely not what Paul was looking for. He never exalted the individual so much that personal rights, thoughts, actions and decisions were of highest importance. Rather, he envisioned the body of Christ as our focus and our highest concern. Often individualism as it occurs in the world is nothing more than blatant self-centeredness.

Look at the four parts of harmony and unity Paul uses. Let's just take the first one for now, "being like-minded." The expression literally means, "think the same thing." Sounds almost communistic, doesn't it?

But that's not Paul's meaning. Think of an orchestra. Each individual plays his own instrument. Some play one melody. Some another. Some only toot a note now and then. Others play at a manic pace through most of the piece. But what is happening overall? As the conductor leads, beautiful strains of music float up and out. It's all synchronized in perfect harmony and unity. Many parts are working together to produce one piece.

What then is it to be of the same mind? It means our minds are all fixed together in making the music work. We submit ourselves to the score, the conductor and the goal. Within those limits, we express ourselves.

MIND: In the same way, think of the Bible as our score, the Holy Spirit as our conductor and the Lord as our audience. By submitting ourselves to the word and the Spirit, we produce a worship that makes the music of heaven, a unified whole, beautiful, resplendent, perfect.

That's unity.

How much did Jesus want that kind of unity? Read about it in John 17:20-23.

MIGHT: Is unity in your church and youth group something you strive after? Is it important to you? What things right now are destroying the unity in your group? What can you personally do this week to counteract them, even provide a healing touch to them?

WEDNESDAY: Maintaining the same love

HEART: Paul's second expression in Philippians is also critical to unity: "having the same love." It literally means, "having the same kind of love—*agape*." It's giving to one another the same level and kind of love—unconditional, unfailing, unearthly love that never quits. Paul said it this way in Ephesians 4:3, "Make every effort to keep the unity of the Spirit through the bond of peace."

That's a pile of words, but notice it has several elements. The first is "making every effort." That's work. It takes cooperation, effort, determination, sweat, blood, tears and toil on everyone's part. Unity doesn't just happen. People—Christians with the Spirit working in them—make it happen.

Then notice Paul says, "Keep the unity of the Spirit." "Keep" means literally to "guard" or "keep watch over." Do you get the idea of someone hovering over it, protecting it from shattering? It's like playing "hot potato." Ever play that? Someone takes a rock or a ball and suddenly it's this hot potato that everybody tosses about trying to pass it on without letting it drop.

SOUL: That's unity. It's a fragile thing. You work at it. Everyone is diligent to keep their love warm towards others. Everyone works to maintain peace and hope. You're all together in this. You look at it as a team or "body" effort.

MIND: Take a look at the kind of unity the church had in Acts 2:46-47 and 4:32. How does that compare with your church situation?

MIGHT: When I was in college, I ran for treasurer of my fraternity. The other candidate and I sat in the basement while the "brothers" talked it out and voted above. Apparently there was much argument for it seemed that we sat down there forever.

Finally, someone came down to talk to me. He asked me what was wrong between me and our house cook.

I had no idea anything was wrong. But apparently our cook had spoken negatively about me for months. In fact, she loathed me. I didn't know there was even a problem. Apparently, one morning I'd said something I'd meant as a joke, but our cook was hurt and angered by it.

I said I'd get it taken care of right away. I was voted in as treasurer.

The next morning, I went into the kitchen and talked to our cook. She forgave me, and after that we became the greatest of friends.

That's maintaining love. That's unity. What can you do to make it happen in your group? Are you angry with anyone? Are you seeking to maintain the spirit and quality of love with everyone?

THURSDAY: Join hands before it's too late.

HEART: Paul concludes with another expression in Philippians, "being one in spirit and purpose." We can mix these things up, but it's clear Paul is concerned about unity, that we all move in the same direction together.

An old rabbi told this story. A new family moved into a community in Minnesota. They were a bit different from the rest and the people there were cold and unfriendly. But one day the new family's six-year-old daughter strayed from the back yard into a wheat field behind the house. The air was cold, and if they did not soon find her, she could die of exposure.

Strangely, the news spread fast and people from all over town came out to help in the search. But they couldn't find her. The air became colder, the new family more desperate.

Then the mayor said, "Let's join hands, form an unbroken line, a human chain, and we will sweep the wheat field before it's too late. We will go up and down until we find the little girl."

In 30 minutes they found her—half frozen, but her heart was still beating. She lived.

At the conclusion of his story, the rabbi said, "I just cannot forget those words of the mayor—'Let's all join hands before it's too late.'"

That's the idea of one purpose. Working towards a goal together and letting nothing stop you.

SOUL: What is our purpose? To glorify the Lord, and enjoy Him and one another forever.

Sometimes churches have "statements of purpose." They might read like this:

"Our purpose is . . .
edification through the Word of God . . .
ministry to one another in the Spirit . . .
reaching the lost and bringing them into
our fellowship."

MIND: Read more about the purpose of the church in such passages as Ephesians 4:11-16, Philippians 2:1-8 and First Corinthians 13:4-8.

MIGHT: What are your personal goals in life? How do they relate to those of Christ and the church as revealed in Scripture? Where do you see that you fit in?

FRIDAY: Four pillars for the building

HEART: We've talked about what unity is. But what is its basis? On what is unity founded?

Again, Paul reveals it in Philippians 2, verse 1: "If you have any encouragement from being united with Christ, if any comfort from his love, if any fellowship with the Spirit, if any tenderness and compassion . . . "

Notice the four pillars:

> encouragement from being united with Christ
> comfort from his love
> fellowship with the Spirit
> tenderness and compassion

SOUL: These aren't difficult concepts. But they're what unity is built on. Without them, unity is impossible. Do you know what destroys these things? They're the very things often found in groups of any kind, adult or youth.

> Gossip
> Jealousy
> Anger
> Immorality
> Impurity
> Self-centeredness
> Disputes
> Factions
> Cliques
> Envy

Love of money
Love of self

Do you see these elements in yourself or in your group?

MIND: Perhaps this is a good time for some self-evaluation. Read the following passages of Scripture with an eye to yourself (not other Christians). As you read, ask the Spirit to point out to you any areas where you personally are sinning. The passages are Galatians 5:19-21, Second Timothy 3:1-7, First Corinthians 13:1-8, Romans 1:28-32. If you find some things you know you're doing, confess them and ask the Lord to help you make things right with anyone you need to.

MIGHT: A musician was giving a brilliant concert for a church audience many years ago. This was in an era when organs produced sound through someone working a pump beneath the floorboards to send air into the pipes. On this occasion, the musician took a break and went down to the pumproom. There he found an old gentleman resting from the hard work of pumping the organ. The old man smiled and said, "We're giving them quite a concert, aren't we?"

The musician immediately felt it necessary to put the gentleman in his place. He said, "What do you mean 'we,' old man? I'm giving the concert."

He went back to the organ and prepared to play again. But when he crashed his hands on the first notes, there was nothing but silence. He dashed back to the pumproom. There was the old man, sitting patiently, but doing no pumping.

A slow smile came onto the musician's lips and he said, "You were right. We are giving them a concert."

Are you thinking in terms of "we" these days, or "I"?

SATURDAY/SUNDAY: The most important thing in the church

HEART: What do you often see happening in the world around us?

From recent headlines in a city newspaper, I can report the following situations taking place in our city and country:

91 military bases and installations will soon be closed down. Why? Not because we want a deeper peace, but because the budget won't support it.

The mayor of Washington, D.C. has been called to account for certain activities in a hotel relating to drugs.

A Pan Am jet crashed in Scotland possibly as the result of a bomb. The FAA will pass into law further security measures to be taken at airports.

An investment firm, Drexel Burnham and Lambert, is under investigation for securities fraud that ranges in the billions of dollars.

Leonid Brezhnev, once the powerful leader of the Soviet Union, has been stripped of all his posthumous honors.

That's a far cry from any semblance of unity.

But is the church any different?

Take a look at the year in the U.S. church. Mention only a few names: Jim and Tammy Bakker; The PTL Club; Jimmy Swaggart. The divorce rate among Christians rising close to the national average. People in the church coming out of the closet about wife abuse, child abuse, homosexuality.

And these are the ones that made headlines.

SOUL: Yet, unity is certainly the most important thing for any Christian group to establish and maintain. Unity demonstrates many things that don't often exist in the outside world:

Genuine love for one another
The fact that God is working in your midst
A picture of the Father, Son and Spirit
The ability to work together towards common goals
Peace
Genuine concern for others

Why does it elude us?

MIND: Where does unity start?

With each of us in our own circle of friends, acquaintances, fellow Christians and relatives. It starts right now with you. And me. It starts where each of us is. If we can't reach unity in that limited circle, what can possibly be done on a larger frame of reference?

How do we gain the unity we crave? Read Romans 15:5-6.

MIGHT: God Himself is the source of unity. We can't establish it on our own. We need His complete and unlimited involvement.

But He always starts somewhere. Perhaps with one person. One Christian working towards unity with others—being of the same mind, maintaining the same love, united in spirit, intent on one purpose.

One person.

Will you give Him leave to start with you? Now?

10

I Just Wish They Wouldn't Stab Me in the Back

Be devoted to one another in brotherly love.
Romans 12:10a

MONDAY: Family

HEART: One of my favorite things about growing up was our many trips to "the Lake." "The Lake" is found in the Poconos of Pennsylvania. It's called Lake Wallenpaupack, and stretches over 13 miles northwest and southeast ending in a dam. It's a man-made lake, the result of damming up the Wallenpaupack River, which empties into the lake at its north end.

What thrilled me about going to the lake was the rousing family times we had in the car. We'd often play games like "Twenty Questions," "Animal, Vegetable, Mineral," and "Beetle" (which was counting the number of Volkswagens on the road). When that lode was exhausted, we'd sing songs. One of Dad's favorites was "The Ship *Titanic*." He'd sing,

When they built the ship Titanic *to sail the ocean
    blue,*
*they thought they had a ship that the water would
    ne'er come through,*
*but 'twas on her maiden trip that an iceberg hit the
    ship,*
it was sad when the great ship went down.
It went down, it went down,
it was sad when the great ship went down—
to the bottom of the—
husbands and wives, little children lost their lives,
it was sad when the great ship went down.

Dad had a little variation. On "little children" in the
last part of the verse, he'd pull his hands off the
wheel and sing in a high, squeaky voice, "little children lost their lives." We'd laugh and cry, "Dad, do it
again, do the part!" He'd do it again, pull his hands
off the wheel, and squeak, "Little children lost their
lives." Meanwhile, my mother would screech, "Dick,
put both hands on the wheel!"

Those were good times, family times, memorable
moments.

SOUL: If there is something all Christians must discover it's the fact that the body of Christ is a family.
We're brothers and sisters, the children of God, His
heirs and His friends. When Paul told the Romans to
"be devoted to one another in brotherly love," he was
thinking of that family atmosphere, that sense of
compassion, tenderness and loyalty you should find
in a home.

Do you have a sense of family around other Christians? Or is a there a distance, a lack of kindness, a destructiveness?

Family life will be the essence of heaven. We'll worship, love and fellowship together forever. If we lack that, though, what is there?

MIND: If you study the families represented in the Bible, you often do not find much by way of happy family life. Abraham and Sarah experienced continual strife between their two sons Ishmael and Isaac. So it was in Isaac's family, too, with Jacob and Esau. Jacob's family even tried to murder Joseph and sold him into slavery. David's family featured a rapist, a murderer and incessant rivalries and intrigues. In fact, there is no family in Scripture that I know of that didn't have problems, breakdowns and disputes.

Why is this? Is this the way it should be? Read some of the principles about how a family should operate in Ephesians 5:22 to 6:4. What insights do you see about how to live as a family in the church?

MIGHT: Several years ago I was with my own family and we reminisced about those years going to the lake. I mentioned all the songs and games we used to play. My mom laughed and said, "Oh, how I hated playing all those dumb games!" I was astonished. "But I thought they were great." She answered, "Oh, we just played them to keep you kids from killing each other in the back seat."

I had to laugh—a little, anyway. But that's a truth

about family life, isn't it? Some members do things for the sake of the others, even when they don't get any immediate reward. That's a part of being "devoted to one another in brotherly love."

TUESDAY: Loyalty

HEART: In yesterday's reading I mentioned the *Titanic*, the famed ship that went down in the North Atlantic on April 15, 1912, after striking an iceberg. Many stories came out of that tragic episode, but one that's always touched me was about an elderly couple on that sinking ship, Mr. and Mrs. Isadore Strauss.

The lifeboats filled up with women and children and repeatedly Mr. Strauss urged his wife to board one. She refused. Finally, he forced her into one and was satisfied. But before she sat down, she jumped up and rushed to his side. She said, "We have been long together through a great many years. We are old now. Where you go, I will go."

SOUL: That's a picture of loyalty. Do you have it? Do you see it in the church? It's part of being devoted to one another. Doing things like:

- Refusing to listen to or pass on rumors about other members.
- Stopping gossip as it firestorms through a group and having nothing to do with it.
- Standing by a friend even when others regard him as different or "uncool."

- Giving what is necessary, even if the recipient has never given back to you.
- Refusing to say nasty things or offer your opinion about someone when you know it would be hurtful.
- Believing the best of people regardless of what others say they have done.

MIND: Read about God's loyal love to us in Romans 5:8 and John 3:16. How loyal was He? When did He do these things—while we were friends or enemies?

MIGHT: Young people often discount the reality of loyalty to others. Yes, they count loyalty to themselves—how other people treat them—very high. But what about showing loyalty yourself—toward your brothers and sisters in Christ? Do you stick up for them? Do you defend the truth even when it hurts? Are you willing to help even when it costs you much in terms of time and money?

WEDNESDAY: Tenderness and compassion

HEART: The Hebrew word for "compassion" is *racham*. It comes from a root which means "womb." I think God linked the two ideas together in Scripture for an important reason: a mother caring for the child of her womb pictures compassion.

Have you seen a mother with a baby lately? Notice how she holds the child, cradles its head, swaddles it in blankets and sleepers, responds to its cries. Notice how her eyes appear as she looks down on that helpless child. That baby is entirely in her hands. She has total power over it. It can do nothing to resist attack or maltreatment.

But God has put within a mother's heart a special brand of compassion and tenderness. And she treats her baby with the highest love and care.

I remember being sick as a child and having my mother nurse me. She'd come upstairs with a tray of chicken noodle soup and toast. She'd cheerily say, "How are you feeling, chickadee—still bum?" She'd sit down on the edge of the bed and watch me eat. It was a tremendously secure feeling to sink deep down under those covers and know that mother was near, caring, ready and eager to help.

SOUL: That's the picture the Lord wants us to have of Him.

Moreover, it's the picture He wants His church to give to the world. He wants it to see our compassion, our care, our devotion to one another. When one is sick, the church members come by to visit, to bring hot food, to chat, to encourage. When one is down, people surround him, eager to touch and build him up.

When I went through a period of depression a number of years ago, it stunned me how my church responded when they learned of my condition. Gifts, letters, phone calls flooded my days. People cared. They were concerned.

And it didn't let up either. It wasn't like they put in their minute and I never saw them again. No, many helped me over and over, even when I was miserable to be around.

MIND: Read Paul's words in First Thessalonians 2:5-9 for some insight into how he treated them when he came to town. Notice his words: they imparted not only the gospel, but "our lives as well." That's the essence of devotion to one another in Christ's name.

MIGHT: Examine your commitment to the body of Christ. Are you devoted to them? Is loving and helping them the essence of your existence? Why or why not?

THURSDAY: Brotherly love

HEART: What is brotherly love? Do you have a brother? Which do you find most prevalent—the love, or the fighting, the disputing, the anger, the brokenness?

All too often that's what we find going on in homes and between brothers today. But what did Paul mean when he spoke of brotherly love?

It might be summed up in a story that comes out of China. A young man committed murder. He fled to his brother's house, stripped off his bloody clothes, dressed in a new shirt and pants, and dashed out into the night. His brother, a Christian, discovered the sin and learned there was a search on for his evil brother. He went to his house and found the clothing and murder weapon among his things. What should

he do? he wondered. Hand it all over to the authorities?

A crowd hurried down the street towards his
house, torches burning brightly. They were carrying a
hangman's rope.

The Christian brother thought quickly, then made
his decision. He dressed in the murderer's bloody
clothing and waited. When the crowd came to his
door, he went without a word and was hanged. He
gave his life so that his sinful brother might live.

SOUL: You don't find that kind of love many places
today. People are caught up in games, greed, pleasure and power—even young people. At the age of ide-
alism, when young people want to save the world,
some in the younger generation have sold out. Many
care only about fast cars, fast bucks and a fast
high.

But real devotion, the kind that springs from
unconditional love, carries a high price tag. It calls for
sacrifice, servanthood, giving all.

MIND: Read Paul's words in Galatians 6:9-10. What
do you think "Let us not become weary in doing
good" means? Do you find it too easy to become
weary, to give up on loving others when they don't
respond to your love? Why or why not?

MIGHT: In the story above, that murderous Chinese
brother came back into the village and learned of
what his brother had done. He felt guilty and broken
about his brother's love for him and he turned him-

self in. But when they took him to the judge, his case was dismissed. "Your brother paid for your crime," he said. "You do not have to pay."

How great a love! Yet, it's the same kind of love that Jesus had for us. He was so devoted to us that He gave His life on our behalf.

In what ways have you been called on this week to give a small part of your life for someone else? Were you willing to give it? Why or why not?

FRIDAY: A little affection

HEART: "Being devoted" to one another involves showing affection to one another. What is affection? "Tender attachment" towards one another. "An emotional commitment to others."

Too often people are unwilling to express real emotion to one another. We don't want to appear sentimental or impassioned. The name of the game is "be cool, be reserved, don't let anyone know you care."

Some years ago a leader at the U.S. Air Force Academy made a study of how cadets fared on the basis of the warmth of their relationships with their parents. The researcher surveyed the parents, asking them how physically affectionate they were with their sons. Then during Parents' Week, he noted which cadets were greeted with bear hugs or arms over the shoulders, and which ones weren't. Over the next three years, all those cadets were rigorously evaluated in leadership ability, psychological stability and dropout rate. It was found that 36 percent of this class eventually dropped out. But cadets whose fathers expressed warmth and love physically had only a seven percent dropout rate. And those who had the closest relationship with their mothers had a dropout rate of 16 percent. Does this tell us something of the human need for affection and love?

SOUL: I think it does. Do you find it difficult to express affection to other people, even members of your family?

> A kind word.
> A compliment.
> A hug.
> A kiss.
> A lengthy embrace.

We need those things in the body of Christ. You need them. I need them. No one should have to ask. We should offer them as part of normal fellowship. There is no reason ever to be ashamed.

MIND: Read the story of Paul and the Ephesian elders in Acts 20:36-38. Remember that we're talking about a group of men here. What is your reaction to this situation?

MIGHT: If you have difficulty expressing affection to others, try it with some "safe" people—your mother, or a grandparent or a brother or sister. Express gratitude, give a compliment, perhaps tell them you love them. When you greet them, try an embrace.

How do you feel about doing such things? Why do you think you feel the way you do?

SATURDAY/SUNDAY: Warmth

HEART:

> I love
> snuggling down under the covers
> finding a cold spot with my foot
> and warming it up.
>
> I love
> lying on the floor
> in front of a fire
> listening to the wood crackle and spit,
> exchanging a word or two
> with my wife,
> watching the colors dance
> and reach
> and lash
> and whip.
>
> I love
> getting into a group of Christians
> over thick-iced chocolate cake
> and coffee
> and vanilla ice cream, people
> who share their feelings,
> answer questions honestly,
> and embrace when we part
> perhaps with a tear.

SOUL: I don't know about you, but I think Christian fellowship can be so beautiful at times.

And at other times, so ugly.

I want it to be beautiful. Always. Don't you?

You want to know how? Be devoted to the people in your group. Expend yourself for them. Give and keep on giving. Reach out. Touch. Express love. Compliment. Share a verse. Talk. Listen.

It's not really complicated.

MIND: Read First Thessalonians 4:9-10 for some insight about love, affection and giving.

MIGHT: This has been a tough week. I've been convicted by the things I've written. I know I don't express affection enough. In fact, sometimes I withhold it from people close to me who need it. Why? Because I'm angry. Or hurt. Or just tired.

You know what? I'm going to resolve to start giving out. Pouring it out. With all my energy. Just love.

Do you think you can do that with me?

11

I Promise I'll Stick with You No Matter What

As a prisoner for the Lord, then, I urge you to live a life worthy of the calling you have received. Be completely humble and gentle; be patient, bearing with one another in love.

Ephesians 4:1-2

MONDAY: Grin and bear it!

HEART: There is an expression I've never liked much: "Just grin and bear it."

I suppose it has something to do with toleration, deciding to find a positive way of looking at a tough situation. But why grin? Why not just bear it?

I guess that's the hard part. It's more than putting on a happy face. I suppose that's the meaning from a worldly point of view. But this is actually something more. It's the determination that I will not allow someone or something to kill my joy. I've determined before the Lord to produce the fruit of joy in my life, and I'm not planning to let anything stop it.

Is that the way you see the idea of grinning and

133

bearing it?

SOUL: What if we changed the expression a little—
"Grin and bear him"(or her). People like:
• Mikie, your little brother who's always hanging
around and wanting to be included, but is just too
young for most of the things you want to do;
• Tim, the guy in church who's a bit obnoxious and
tends to say embarrassing things, like, "You'd better
do something about that pimple today";
• that grandmother or great aunt who always has a
criticism about you, your hair, your clothing, your
music;
• that youth minister who's terribly uncool, totally
unlike the guy at the church up the street who
seems to have just the right touch;
• that parent who is always nagging;
• that pastor who is always stretching his sermon
past the allotted time.
What do you do with such people? Grin and bear
them.

MIND: Paul stated the principle in Ephesians 4:2:
"bearing with one another in love." Read that passage today in Ephesians 4:1-6. What do you think is
Paul's primary concern here? What does "bearing
with" mean?

MIGHT: Actually, it means to endure, or literally,
"put up with." Do you ever have to "put up with"
someone? "Put up with one another," says Paul.
That's classic. You wouldn't normally think of a

proper Christian attitude as "putting up with some-one." You usually say it with a little sigh.

"Well, I guess I can put up with him for an hour or so."

"All right. I'll put up with him this time. But next time, watch out!"

"Can't you put up with her for a little while, honey? She's only here for a few hours."

Yet, that's a true Christian attitude we're to have with sometimes obnoxious, sometimes noxious and sometimes toxic people! We're to be tolerant, to overlook, to endure with them even though some-times we'd much rather they didn't exist.

TUESDAY: Putting up with someone

HEART: I'd like to ask you to bear with me for a moment. Go back and read yesterday's reading. Did anything about it trouble you—especially the part about putting up with certain people? Does that seem like a truly Christian way of looking at oth-ers?

You know, one thing I've heard a lot as a Christian is the idea of "loving someone in Jesus." In essence, the idea is that you can't quite love them for their own sake, or you can't generate your own decent feel-ings towards them, so somehow you buck up and "love them in Jesus." Oh, you'd never tell them that (unless you wanted to be truly obnoxious—"Bill, I can't love you myself, so I'm praying that Jesus will help me love you"—something just doesn't sound right about that), but sometimes you wish you could.

Yet, have you ever noticed how different we all are? Each of us has habits, idiosyncrasies, special little elements of our personalities that literally "turn people off."

"He just turns me off." "She's such a downer." Those are expressions I used to use. Do you have any of your own?

SOUL: You get the point. There are some of us out there who

- smell
- have bad breath
- dress like a nerd
- always say the wrong thing at the wrong time
- can't seem to get the message when you want us to go away
- have a way of ruining the evening every time
- are "gross"
- you wish would just go away . . . forever

What do you do with those people? Put an anonymous note in their mailbox? Lose your head and start screaming at them on the bus? Report them to the principal? Discuss them with your guidance counselor?

Paul says, "Put up with them."

Isn't that astonishing? He doesn't say, "Love them in Jesus." He doesn't say, "Ask the Lord to change your heart towards them." He doesn't say, "Pray that God will change them into someone more likable."

He says, "Put up with them."

MIND: I like that. It means I don't have to pretend. It means I don't have to work up some "Christian" feeling that is supposedly more spiritual. It means I don't have to tell lies so no one knows how I really feel.

No, it means "hanging in there" with them, praying for them, treating them with dignity and kindness even when you don't feel like it. Respecting them as people made in the image of God.

But it doesn't mean being dishonest, faking it, or going out of your way to be "extra nice" as a cover-up.

The Scriptures are so practical, aren't they? Read a story about how Jesus "put up with some people" we call the disciples—Mark 9:14-29, with special emphasis on Mark 9:19. Even Jesus felt that way at times!

MIGHT: One thing I've learned in my few years as a Christian—there are some people you meet that you will never truly "like." It's just something about our humanness that makes us selective in whom we can give ourselves to. But you know what? If we try, we can "put up with" just about anyone or anything, if we work at it "in Jesus." And we can do it out of love for Him, for the truth and for the person we have to endure. Right?

Whom are you struggling to "put up with" now? Ask the Lord to help you to "be patient, bearing with one another in love."

WEDNESDAY: Mercy and loyalty

HEART: Perhaps you've heard of the scandal 20 years ago that destroyed the presidential administration of Richard Nixon. It was called Watergate because five followers of Nixon broke into the Democratic National Headquarters in the Watergate building on June 17, 1972, to burglarize it. Eventually, the commander behind the team was traced to Nixon himself. He resigned in shame and degradation.

But out of Watergate, several people became Christians, among them Charles Colson, once known as Nixon's "hatchet man." He went to prison and later founded an outreach and training organization for prisoners called *Prison Fellowship*. Colson now travels about the world speaking on behalf of prison reform and Jesus Christ.

SOUL: Some years ago, in 1979, with Watergate in the past but still much in the minds of many, Colson spoke on a college campus, giving his testimony. A question and answer period followed in which many students asked about his involvement in the scandal. The audience was hostile. The questions were tinged with anger, even hatred. Finally, one enraged student stood and challenged Colson about the whole nature of his relationship with Nixon, now fallen and in seclusion in California.

Colson hesitated to answer. It was a perfect moment for him once and for all to disown his mentor and be rid of his ghost forever. The audience waited. Many faces were sweaty and red with anger.

Then he spoke quietly but decisively into the microphone. He said, "Richard Nixon is my friend."

What would you expect to happen? The wrath of the whole body turned on Colson? Perhaps a riot? Maybe even something close to a lynching?

Nothing of the above. The student body erupted into spontaneous applause, some of them even standing. Colson had touched something deep down in all of us that we consider paramount. The word is loyalty.

MIND: Loyalty is an element of bearing with one another. So is mercy. In that moment on that podium, Colson did not diminish at all. Rather, his mercy towards Nixon, and his obvious loyalty said something strong and deep to that audience.

Are you loyal? Are you merciful to those Christians about you who don't seem to "measure up?" Read about a time when Jesus was merciful to someone who had denied he even knew Him—Peter in John 21:15-23. Why do you think Jesus asked the questions He did? Why was His approach loyal, even merciful?

MIGHT: Mercy is tough. Loyalty is tougher. How do you stick by someone when they've totally blown it? When everyone else rejects them?

Have you had such an opportunity recently? Do you have one now? How are you doing? Are you showing loyalty, or are you deserting them in the crush? Are you willing to be forbearing even when they have done something terribly wrong?

THURSDAY: The milk of human kindness

HEART: I was certain the young man sitting in my kitchen would rip me off. He needed $40. He would repay it, he said, in a week. He would soon be starting a new job.

He told me about himself. He'd been in a mental hospital for some time. He had a fetish for women's hair. I didn't understand what that meant. He kept coming back to his need of $40.

I gave it to him. A check.

I never saw him again.

SOUL: It's not like it's happened only once either.

There was Lisa. She needed money to pay the rent—$300. We'd already caught her once cohabiting with her boyfriend. But they'd finally gotten married. They promised to come to church, live right, walk with the Lord.

We gave them the $300.

They never came back.

Then there was Mrs. Corren. She called up the church one Sunday afternoon. It was January. Frigid out. They were going to shut off her heat. She needed $60. Her daughter was undergoing "creamatherapy" (as she called it—little did I know that I was the one getting "creamed") for cancer. Had lost all her hair.

I talked to the deacons. We gave her the money.

With it, I gave her a tract. She was thankful. She praised Jesus.

The next week she needed more—$90 this time.

Three days later she needed more—$150—"or they'll put me out on the street."

That's when I started to investigate. Seems Mrs. Corren had made the rounds of all the churches. "She's the perfect con artist," one pastor told me.

I refused to give her any more money.

She pled with me.

I told her no.

She began weeping. "My baby, my baby will die of cancer."

I was astonished. In the end, we refused to help her any more. We were already into her for nearly $400.

So I wondered, *would all these cons make me refuse to help the next guy, who might be on the level?*

Well, it has made me more cautious. But then again, I remember how many times others have helped me, and I didn't do much of anything in return.

MIND: Ever feel like that—always giving out, and getting nothing in return?

It happens. Jesus is the supreme example. There are people—even Christians—who will use you, abuse you, confuse you, refuse you—even after you've given all to them.

What do you do with them? Look at Jesus and Judas Iscariot in John 12:1-8. How long did Jesus bear with Judas, knowing, even from the beginning, that he was a rascal?

MIGHT: Kindness is part of "bearing with" someone. It's the positive side of it. In one sense you can "put up with someone." In another sense, you "do for them." You act in kindness. You treat them kindly, even though you may know they will give you nothing in return.

Do you have a Christian friend who's always taking and never giving, perhaps is even a "con artist?" How should you treat them? What steps can you take now to work with them, even endure knowing they may never change?

FRIDAY: A little personal attention, please

HEART: Ever memorize sick jokes? I did, in ninth grade. I remember a few today. Here's my favorite:

> *Little Willie with a shout,*
> *Gouged the baby's eyeballs out.*
> *Stamped on them to make them pop.*
> *Mother cried, "Now, William, stop!"*

Oh, that's awful! Absolutely gross. Revolting.
But some of us laugh anyway.
Perhaps I'm a paragon of evil, but do you know at times that I've thought of that poem when I'm engrossed in a book and my five-year-old daughter comes over to the couch asking me to read her a

book or play with her Barbie dolls.

How I hate Barbie dolls! She wants me to talk to them, and carry on a conversation and have them sit in their little chairs.

Ugh!

SOUL: It's so hard. But when I put her off long enough, someone usually tells me, "Mark, she's going to grow up and reach 16 and then you'll want her to talk to you and she won't be interested."

So I stop my reading, pick up a Barbie doll, and say, "Hi, my name's Oogal-doogal, what's yours?"

"Her name's not Oogullie-doogal, Daddy. Come on. Play right."

"Look, kid," I feel like saying, "you've got me this far, don't press your luck." But I don't. I just shrug, grit my teeth and say, "Oh, you look so nice today, Barbie, don't you think you should put on your clothes?"

"Yes," my daughter answers in her special Barbie voice. "Will you help me?"

(Why is it that the first thing a little girl does to a doll is strip her?)

MIND: Personal attention. That's part of bearing with your Christian brethren, isn't it? Like listening, really listening—to every word—even when the person speaking is so dull you'd rather go memorize the phone book. That means playing, really getting into it, even when your heart is screaming, "I want to read my book." It calls for spending time with the other party, even when you'd rather part.

Take a look at Jesus on the busiest day of His life recorded in Scripture—Mark 1:21-34. What had He been doing all day? Do you think He might have been tired on occasion, or that He desired a little time to Himself?

MIGHT: Bearing with those around us is one of life's most difficult problems. Some of us are so self-absorbed, aren't we? We have all our little projects, games, books and things we want to do. And then there's this creep, Willie, who comes along and wants to steal our time with his nonsense.

What will you do with him? How can you cope?

SATURDAY/SUNDAY:
"Quit feeding off me!"

HEART: There was a movie years ago called, *Cool Hand Luke*. It starred Paul Newman and was about a man in a work prison in the South who couldn't seem to cooperate with the authorities. A famous quote came out of that movie about the problem Luke had in listening to the warden. After escaping twice, the warden utters the classic line: "What we got here is a failure to communicate." However, Luke's capers, playfulness and sheer dogged unwillingness to succumb to anything wins the hearts of his fellow prisoners. They look up to him as a kind of leader, almost a god.

But another classic moment occurred in the movie when Luke rebelled even against his admirers' admiration. After suffering numerous blows and failures, and even cooking in solitary confinement for several days because of his rebelliousness, Luke responds to his peers' admiration and love with the words, "Quit feeding off of me!"

SOUL: I've often thought about that line as a Christian, for I've found that there are many Christians who, in a sense, "feed off" one another. Certain leaders and standout Christians seem to possess an aura, a power, an inexplicable strength that others find encouraging and uplifting. They're attracted to it like metal specks to a magnet.

In a sense, we feed off such Christians. They're the dynamic leaders, the inextinguishable lights among us.

We have to deal with such attitudes. Do you find yourself ever feeling like one of those who seems to attract lots of friends, people who depend on you, want you, want your time, people who seem to "feed" off of you, your soul, your very being?

MIND: It can get tiring. Like Cool Hand Luke above, you can get to the point where you rebel.

But Jesus never did. In fact, He wants us to feed off of Him. "I am the bread of life," He said. What was the secret of Jesus' power? Read about it in Mark 1:35-39. What does this passage reveal as the source of Jesus' incredible power to endure even when the mob pressed in upon Him?

MIGHT: Do you find yourself tired, wrung out, wishing everyone would just leave you alone? We all need solitude. But we especially need time alone with the Lord, time to feed off of Him. It's only through such time that we gain the power to "forbear" with the many who make demands upon us.

Are you spending time in prayer and study? I suppose if you're reading this book and taking it seriously, you are. I hope so. It's only through the Lord that any of us has anything good to do, say or think about anyone. Remember Jesus' dictum, "apart from me, you can do nothing" (John 15:5). Why not memorize that passage and meditate on it as a guide for the source of the power to live up to all these "one another" ideas we've been talking about?

12

I'll Love You to the End of Time

A new command I give to you: Love one another. As I have loved you, so you must love one another.
John 13:34

MONDAY: A new commandment

HEART: Why does Jesus call loving one another as He loved us a "new" command?

The word used here for new is *kainos*. This word means new in the sense of something never seen before, something you personally are unaccustomed to, new in terms of quality and of a different form from what is old and known.

Then how is this kind of love "new"?

It's new in the sense that it's been personally demonstrated to us by Jesus. We never saw love of this brand before. Just before speaking those words in John 13:34-35, what had Jesus done? He'd washed the disciples' feet. The King of glory stepped down off His high and glorious throne, put on a towel, knelt down before 12 different men (including the one who would betray Him), and carefully wiped the scum off each foot and between the toes.

How would you like doing that? Does it make you want to throw up?

Maybe Jesus felt that way, too. But He still did the job. He got it done. He didn't flinch, whimper or say, "I'm doing this because My Father made Me." He did it as an example, because He had the heart of a servant and because He loved those 12 and every other person down to you and me.

SOUL: Perhaps that puts a new wrinkle on the whole, "love one another" trip for you. It does for me.

Love others? "Sure, why I gave 10 percent last week in church. I helped out in the class. I gave a word of encouragement to the pastor on the way out the door. In school, I even spoke to that nerd, Bill James without grimacing."

On the other hand, there's Jesus.

He sacrificed His time continually in order to heal, preach and disciple.

He sacrificed a warm bed and regular hot meals to go out into the countryside and travel city to city, house to house, helping, healing, loving, encouraging.

He sacrificed His right to be worshiped and loved by giving up His rights and walking among men, only to be rejected and hated.

He sacrificed His position of power to wash men's feet.

He sacrificed His right to a just trial.

He sacrificed His dignity by allowing sinful people

to put a crown of thorns on His head and mock Him in a purple robe.

He sacrificed His blood, His life, His fellowship with the Father, to save us.

Look at His whole life. It goes from sacrifice to sacrifice. Each is significant. Each is memorable. Each was selfless.

And what about you and me?

MIND: Read about God's love in an often-memorized verse, Romans 5:8. Concentrate on the word "demonstrates" and visualize what that entailed.

MIGHT: Do you love others? Do you really care?

I know. I'm getting preachy. In fact, I'm preaching to myself. Sometimes I wake up and realize I'm a selfish, self-centered, egotistical, unfeeling dog. But then someone says, "Fetch!" and I wag my tail and do it without a complaint. Then suddenly I feel like a real GOOD Christian!

Just the same, love is hard, isn't it? Most of us do well with words. We can say, "I love you" with the best of them. But it's action that counts. Are you willing to take action—on behalf of another—in love?

That's the test of your Christianity.

TUESDAY: Lights, camera, action!

HEART: In yesterday's reading I mentioned action as the essence of love. Love acts. It does things. It labors. It travails. It not only cares, but like the Good Samaritan, it chooses to show its care with deeds.

Bob Rowland once paraphrased Matthew 25:35-36 with these words:

I was hungry, and you formed a humanities club and discussed my hunger. Thank you.

I was imprisoned, and you crept off quietly to your chapel in the cellar and prayed for my release.

I was naked, and in your mind you debated the morality of my appearance.

I was sick, and you knelt and thanked God for your health.

I was homeless, and you preached to me of the spiritual shelter of the love of God.

I was lonely, and you left me alone to pray for me.

You seem so holy; so close to God. But I'm still very hungry, and lonely, and cold.

SOUL: Is that the way too many of us Christians show our "love"? Is that even love to begin with?

No. Never. God did not just say He loves us. He came down among us, healed, walked the streets with us, listened, spent time, sought to understand, looked into the depths of our hearts and unstrung the cries that were tied there.

Whom do you know who needs a little love? Or a lot? Are you willing to sacrifice for them? Are you willing to go the extra mile, or five miles, or 10? Are you willing to take off your new designer shirt and clothe them in it?

MIND: Read a little more about love in Matthew 25:31-46. Do you find Jesus' words graphic? Practical?

Applicable to your life today?

MIGHT: You don't find such love often in our world today. In fact, one of the signs of the last times, Jesus said, would be the fact that many people's love will grow cold (Matthew 24:12). Do you see that coldness around you? In your family? Your church? The department store? The parking lot? The highway? The classroom? What can you do today to warm it up a little?

WEDNESDAY: Vulnerability

HEART: In 1967 a first happened in pro football. Gale Sayers, a black man, and Brian Piccolo, a white man, were paired together as roommates. For each man it was also a first. Piccolo had never experienced intimacy with a black person before. Nor had Sayers with a white person.

Nonetheless, as fellow running backs on the Chicago Bears, they developed a fierce commitment to one another. On the playing field, and off. Their friendship grew as one of the best relationships in pro sports. They were inseparable, and each made sacrifices for the other. They were developing as the Dynamic Duo of the Bears' backfield.

Then, in 1969, Piccolo began to slow down, suffering from frequent ailments. After some stiff examinations, the doctors told him he had incurable cancer. He didn't have long to live.

Piccolo rebounded several times and fought to stay in the starting 11 in the 1969 season. But he spent most of his time in a hospital bed in pain and frustration.

Toward the end of the season, Sayers was given the George S. Halas Award for being the most courageous player in pro football. As he stood at the podium to accept, Sayers said, "You flatter me by giving me this award."

His voice was strained. Tears were in his eyes. But he continued. "But I tell you here and now that I accept it for Brian Piccolo. He is the man of courage who should receive the George S. Halas Award."

He paused, then concluded, "I love Brian Piccolo."

SOUL: Perhaps that was the greatest act of courage of all. So simple. Yet so beautiful.

And so unusual.

Why? Why are we so touched by such a tribute? Perhaps because of its emotion. Perhaps because of the situation. Perhaps because of the racial implications.

But I think it's something more. It has something to do with the volunteer element of love. No one forced Sayers to say that. No one put a gun to his head, and said, "Give it to Piccolo." No one programmed him like a computer so that the words came up at the flick of a switch.

It was totally of himself. Given freely, sincerely, unashamedly.

MIND: Can you offer love like that? Can you say, "I love you," in public, or even in private, to those dear to you? Can you take that action which might make you entirely vulnerable to another's rejection, and yet do it anyway?

Read about how Jesus explained love to some people totally void of it. You'll find His words in Luke 15:1-32 where He tells three parables about what God does to show us His love.

MIGHT: To whom do you need to say, "I love you"? Take that step. Today.

THURSDAY: A sweet old man

HEART: I once heard Grady Wilson, one of Billy Graham's co-evangelists, tell the story of Uncle Buddy Robinson. Seems Uncle Buddy was feeling ill in his old age and went to a doctor to find out what was wrong. The doctor said he had diabetes.

"Well, what's that?" Uncle Buddy asked.

The doctor answered, "It means you have too much sugar in your blood."

Uncle Buddy jumped up. "Well, praise the Lord!"

The doc stared at him and Uncle Buddy explained. "I been praying that the Lord would make me a sweet old man. And He overdone it!"

SOUL: A sweet old man!

Not many around these days.

Or sweet young men.

Or sweet middle-aged men.

Or sweet any men.

So many of us are tearing through this world, bent on making our mark, ambition oozing from every pore. I'm not just talking about people like me, nailed deep in the barnwood of Yuppiedom. You even see it in young people—high school and college age. A grit-teeth determination to make it big. Eyes fixed on a law practice, or on medicine or business. Making a buck. Making lots of bucks. Making your mark as someone important.

But what mark are you leaving on those around you—Mom, Dad, Sis, Bro, the group at church, the kids in school? Is there a burnt-out strip on the minds of those who know you? Or a memory, filled with sweetness and joy?

MIND: It's hard to get the world's idea of importance out of our minds. We think of it in terms of dollar signs. But do you ever think about just being a sweet young man or woman? Someone whom people enjoy, love and find full of the Spirit and of wisdom? Read about something a sweet old man might do in love which pleases God. You'll find it in Matthew 10:42.

MIGHT: If we could strip your body away and look deep into your soul, what would we see—sweetness or muck? Only you know the answer. Take a hard look at how you treat other people, at the things that go on in your mind and heart. Then read Matthew 7:12 and ask yourself several times when you're with a group, "How would I want to be treated?" Then go and treat someone that way.

FRIDAY: Love in the little things

HEART:
I envision it this way:

The house is burning.
Rooms in flames.
I leap through a hoop of fire,
singeing my arms.
I brush it off, set my lips, and run through a
     wall
of flames to rescue
the baby.
When I stagger out into the firemen's arms,
everyone is congratulating me.
"What a hero!" "What courage!"

Or the car careens down the street.
The little girl's playing in a mud puddle.
The driver doesn't see her.
I leap, and cast her out of the way.
The tires crunch over my back.
In the hospital
the parents thank me. The little girl
gives me a hug.

Or it's on a plane. The terrorist
threatens to take two servicemen.
They'll shoot them and throw them out.
But I stand up.
"Take me. Shoot me in their place.
I'm a Christian. I know where I'll go."

They take me.
I arrive in heaven to angelic music.

But mostly, mostly
it's staying an extra hour with Grandpop
in the nursing home
it's finishing the lawnmowing
with a smile
it's playing her music when I'd rather
listen to my music.

It's the little things.
But they add up.

SOUL: Ever think of love like that?

We picture the grand moments, don't we? Something heroic. Unforgettable. A once-in-a-lifetime chance at proving once and for all you're really a decent, loving guy after all.

But it doesn't happen like that.

I often think of love as giving of yourself in the little moments.

• Replacing the empty toilet paper with a new roll instead of leaving it for Mom.

• Offering to help clear the table without so much as a prod or suggestion from Dad.

• Striving to keep your room neat—just for Mom—for a week.

• Giving up the bigger piece of cake to your little brother.

• Watching the dumb game show instead of the

teen movie because Grandmom likes it so much.

• Listening to Grandpop tell that same story for the 80th time and still laughing anyway because you know how much he likes it when you do.

• Not complaining even in your mind when Mom asks you to go to the store and pick up something she forgot and you'd rather see "The Cosby Show."

MIND: What do you think? Isn't love made up of a multitude of little acts and gifts every day? Or do we have to wait for the grand gesture to prove it once and for all?

Read an interesting example of what love involved in Acts 6:1-7 when the Greek widows were being mistreated.

MIGHT: What little things can you do today that show love?

Here's a suggestion. Before you act or speak in regard to anything, ask yourself, "What is the loving thing to do?" Once you've answered, the only question left is, "Will you do it?"

SATURDAY/SUNDAY:
A treasure of words

HEART: People pressed in about me. It was the end of my summer in 1975, the end of the greatest ministry I'd had since I entered seminary. I hardly noticed the little yellow three by five card one of the eighth-grade girls thrust into my hand. I read it later. She expressed kind and encouraging thoughts about my ministry that summer in Hershey, Pennsylvania. I put the note among some other keepsakes.

That fall something sinister twisted inside my soul and I slipped into a deep, black depression. It was to last two and a half years. At times I was suicidal, feeling God had deserted me, rejected me. I couldn't minister, couldn't speak in public anymore. The one Bible study I was teaching was boring, losing members weekly. I felt as though my life was finished and all I had to do was wait for God to take me home.

But one day in the midst of the darkness I opened the little notebook of keepsakes from that church in Hershey. I came across Meta's note, taped to one of the pages.

SOUL: It read:

"Dear Mark, I'm one of those emotional types, so I wrote what I wanted to say on this card. I'm afraid I'd cry if I said it out loud.

"I wish you weren't leaving. But since you have to, good luck.

"A few weeks ago we came to Wednesday night Bible Study and my brother was making his usual remarks, how boring it would be. But you were teaching, and believe it or not he came home full of talk about it. And now he comes all the time.

"I didn't know you were studying to be a minister until tonight. But I know you'll make it and be a great one.

"Love in Jesus, Meta."

I stared at those words, stunned, weak, on the edge of tears. Then I read it again. And again.

After that I put it in my wallet and kept it there to take out at opportune moments.

MIND: A small act of kindness. It became a wall that held me back from self-pity, self-hatred and suicide. It became a prod to keep me running the race. It was gold for the soul—a treasure of words.

You have such words. And they cost you nothing. But for someone else they might be diamonds, each one worth millions.

Read about the things you can do to show more love to others in Romans 12:9-21.

MIGHT: We've come to the end of this book. It's been an adventure for me to write it. I hope it's been that way for you to read it. But the important thing is that we both go and practice the truths imbedded in it. To

- Act like we really belong to one another
- Accept one another
- Honor one another
- Confess our sins to one another
- Serve one another
- Encourage one another
- Submit to one another
- Admonish one another
- Be of the same mind with one another
- Be devoted to one another
- Bear with one another

and
- LOVE one another, always and forever.

Is this your passion, your hope, your goal?
Then let's covenant together now to make it the expression of our lives.